National Curriculum Standards for Social Studies

I Culture

Social studies programs should include experiences that provide for the study of culture and cultural diversity.

II Time, Continuity, & Change

Social studies programs should include experiences that provide for the study of the ways human beings view themselves in and over time while recognizing examples of change and cause and effect relationships.

III People, Places, & Environments

Social studies programs should include experiences that provide for the study of people, places, and environments.

IV Individual Development & Identity

Social studies programs should include experiences that provide for the study of individual development and identity while recognizing personal changes over time and personal connections to places.

V Individuals, Groups, & Institutions

Social studies programs should include experiences that provide for the study of interactions among individuals, groups, and institutions while giving examples of and explaining, group and institutional influences on people, events, and elements of culture.

VI Power, Authority, & Governance

Social studies programs should include experiences that provide for the study of how people create and change structures of power, authority, and governance while examining the rights and responsibilities of the individual in relation to his or her social group.

VII Production, Distribution, & Consumption

Social studies programs should include experiences that provide for the study of how people organize for the production, distribution, and consumption of goods and services.

VIII Science, Technology, & Society

Social studies programs should include experiences that provide for the study of relationships among science, technology, and society.

IX Global Connections

Social studies programs should include experiences that provide for the study of global connections and independence while giving examples of conflict, cooperation, and interdependence among individuals, groups, and nations.

X Civic Ideals & Practices

Social studies programs should include experiences that provide for the study of the ideals, principles, and practices of citizenship in a democratic republic.

National Geography Standards

The *Geographically Informed Person* knows and understands . . .

THE WORLD IN SPATIAL TERMS

STANDARD 1: How to use maps and other geographic representations, tools, and technologies to acquire, process, and report information.

STANDARD 2: How to use mental maps to organize information about people, places, and environments.

STANDARD 3: How to analyze the spatial organization of people, places, and environments on Earth's surface.

PLACES AND REGIONS

STANDARD 4: The physical and human characteristics of places.

STANDARD 5: That people create regions to interpret Earth's complexity.

STANDARD 6: How culture and experience influence people's perception of places and regions.

PHYSICAL SYSTEMS

STANDARD 7: The physical processes that shape the patterns of Earth's surface.

STANDARD 8: The characteristics and spatial distribution of ecosystems on Earth's surface.

HUMAN SYSTEMS

STANDARD 9: The characteristics, distribution, and migration of human populations on Earth's surface.

STANDARD 10: The characteristics, distributions, and complexity of Earth's cultural mosaics.

STANDARD 11: The patterns and networks of economic interdependence on Earth's surface.

STANDARD 12: The process, patterns, and functions of human settlement.

STANDARD 13: How forces of cooperation and conflict among people influence the division and control of Earth's surface.

ENVIRONMENT AND SOCIETY

STANDARD 14: How human actions modify the physical environment.

STANDARD 15: How physical systems affect human systems.

STANDARD 16: The changes that occur in the meaning, use, distribution, and importance of resources.

THE USES OF GEOGRAPHY

STANDARD 17: How to apply geography to interpret the past.

STANDARD 18: To apply geography to interpret the present and plan for the future.

Macmillan/McGraw-Hill TIMELINKS

Our Country and Its Regions

PROGRAM AUTHORS

James A. Banks
Kevin P. Colleary
Linda Greenow
Walter C. Parker
Emily M. Schell
Dinah Zike

CONTRIBUTORS

Raymond C. Jones
Irma M. Olmedo

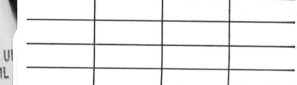

DATE DUE

DEMCO

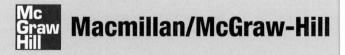

Mc Graw Hill **Macmillan/McGraw-Hill**

Volume I

PROGRAM AUTHORS

James A. Banks, Ph.D.
Kerry and Linda Killinger
  Professor of Diversity Studies
  and Director, Center for
  Multicultural Education
University of Washington
Seattle, Washington

Kevin P. Colleary, Ed.D.
Curriculum and Teaching
  Department
Graduate School of Education
Fordham University
New York, New York

Linda Greenow, Ph.D.
Associate Professor and Chair
Department of Geography
State University of New York at
  New Paltz
New Paltz, New York

Walter C. Parker, Ph.D.
Professor of Social Studies
  Education, Adjunct Professor
  of Political Science
University of Washington
Seattle, Washington

Emily M. Schell, Ed.D.
Visiting Professor, Teacher
  Education
San Diego State University
San Diego, California

Dinah Zike
Educational Consultant
Dinah-Mite Activities, Inc.
San Antonio, Texas

CONTRIBUTORS

Raymond C. Jones, Ph.D.
Director of Secondary Social
  Studies Education
Wake Forest University
Winston-Salem, North Carolina

Irma M. Olmedo
Associate Professor
University of Illinois-Chicago
College of Education
Chicago, Illinois

HISTORIANS/SCHOLARS

Ned Blackhawk
Associate Professor of History
  and American Indian Studies
University of Wisconsin
Madison, Wisconsin

Sheilah F. Clarke-Ekong, Ph.D.
Professor of Anthropology
University of Missouri-St. Louis
St. Louis, Missouri

Larry Dale, Ph.D.
Director, Center for Economic
  Education
Arkansas State University
Jonesboro, Arkansas

Brooks Green, Ph.D.
Associate Professor of
  Geography
University of Central Arkansas
Conway, Arkansas

Thomas C. Holt, Ph.D.
Professor of History
University of Chicago
Chicago, Illinois

 **RFB&D** learning through listening

Students with print disabilities may be eligible to obtain an accessible, audio version of the pupil edition of this textbook. Please call Recording for the Blind & Dyslexic at 1-800-221-4792 for complete information.

The McGraw·Hill Companies

 **Macmillan
McGraw-Hill**

Send all inquires to:
Macmillan/McGraw-Hill
8787 Orion Place
Columbus, OH 43240-4027

MHID 0-02-151347-3
ISBN 978-0-02-151347-5
Printed in the United States of America.
5 6 7 8 9 10 DOW 13 12 11 10

Our Country and Its Regions

CONTENTS, Volume 1

Unit 2 The United States: Its Land and People 65

How do people meet their needs?

Reference Section

Skills and Features

Maps

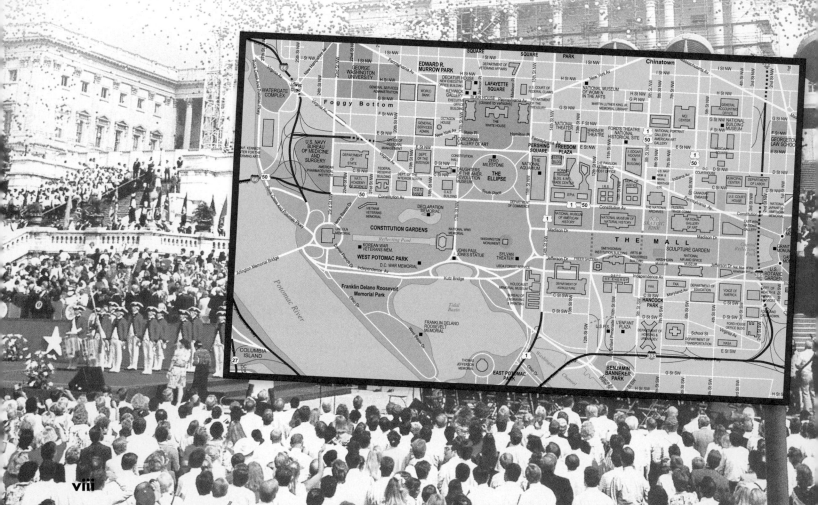

Our National Story

Unit 1

EXPLORE The Big Idea

Essential Question
What are some events that have shaped our nation?

Sequencing Events
Use the time line as you read this unit. Write **Our National Story** at the top. Label the sections **The First Americans, Three Worlds Meet, A Nation is Born, The Nation Grows, War and Changes, A Changing World, A Modern World**. Use the foldable to enter important events and their dates as you read.

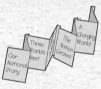

LOG ON
For more about Unit 1 go to
www.macmillanmh.com

Washington, D.C.

1

PEOPLE, PLACES, AND EVENTS

The Founders

Independence Hall

The Founders gathered at **Independence Hall** on May 25, 1787, to create the government of the United States.

Today you can visit Independence Hall in Philadelphia, Pennsylvania.

Dr. Martin Luther King, Jr.

March on Washington

On August 28, 1963, more than 250,000 people listened to **Dr. Martin Luther King, Jr.,** give a speech about civil rights during the **March on Washington**.

Today you can learn more about Dr. Martin Luther King, Jr., at The King Center in Atlanta, Georgia.

Gettysburg

Drummer Boy

The Civil War is the only war to have been fought between Americans in America. Over 3 million people battled in the 4-year-long war. Young boys joined the war as **drummer boys**.

Today you can visit the Civil War battlefield at **Gettysburg,** Pennsylvania.

US Space and Rocket Center

Neil Armstrong and Buzz Aldrin

On July 16, 1969, the United States sent its first manned spacecraft to the moon. **Neil Armstrong and Buzz Aldrin** became the first Americans on the moon.

Today you can learn more about the space program at the **US Space and Rocket Center** in Huntsville, Alabama.

Why Study History?

Why do you watch movies or read novels? Could it be because they're fun and you like a good story? Reading about history is nearly the same thing. The one big difference is that history really happened.

Learning about the past is not only fun, it also helps you understand the world you live in today. For example, do you know why we celebrate Thanksgiving every year? No? Well, keep reading to find out. The more history you know, the better you'll understand how the world around you was put together. That can make every day a little more interesting.

Family photographs are part of history.

Sources of the Past

You can learn about and create history in different ways. When you write something in a diary, take a photograph, or draw a picture, you're making history. This is also how we learn about the past. Have you ever found an old coin or looked at an old photograph? Why are these things so interesting? Because they are clues to the past.

Just as you are making history by leaving clues for people many years from now, you can learn about the past from people who have left clues for you. To learn about their experiences, you can read their words in diaries, letters, old newspapers, and look at their photographs.

Old photographs are part of history.

History All Around Us

One of the most amazing things is that history is something that all Americans share. Whether your family came to this country yesterday or long ago; whether they are African American, white, Native American, Hispanic, or Asian, the history of the United States is their history, too.

New photographs are part of history.

Americans of all backgrounds share a history.

Chart and Graph Skills

Read a Time Line

To understand history, it is important to know when events happened. Sometimes it is not easy to remember what happened first, next, and last. A time line can help sequence events. A time line is a diagram that shows the order of events in history. It also shows the amount of time that passed between events. This helps to give a sense of order to history.

1540 Spanish explorer Francisco Coronado's army marches into the area of present-day Texas

1500   1550   1600

1520 Spanish explorer Alonso Alvarez de Piñeda sails along a river in Mexico

1607 Jamestown, Virginia becomes the first permanent English settlement

Learn It

- Time lines are divided into parts. Each part represents a certain number of years. The time line on this page is divided into parts 50 years long. It tells of the first explorers, settlements, and colonies over a period of 200 years.

- Read the captions from left to right. You can see that the earliest event happened to the left and the latest event happened on the right. On this time line, the first explorer came to Mexico in 1520. When was the last settlement in this time period founded?

Try It

Look at the time line to answer the questions.

- Did French explorers or Spanish explorers reach the Southwest first?

- Did Coronado's army march into Texas before or after de La Salle built a colony on the Texas coast?

Apply It

Use the time line on this page to answer the question below.

- Find important dates of your life by talking with family members.

- Find an important event for each year. Try to draw a picture or place a photograph for each event. Make a time line of your life.

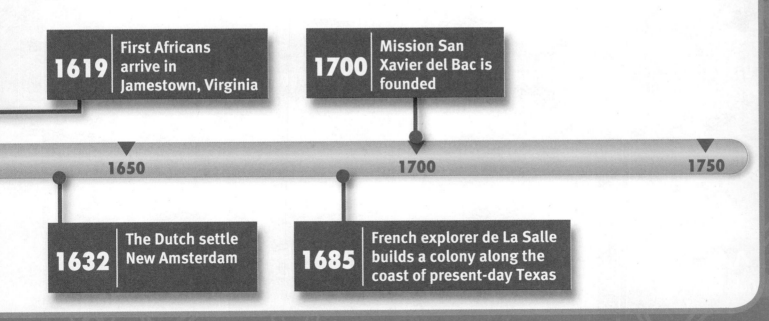

1619 First Africans arrive in Jamestown, Virginia

1700 Mission San Xavier del Bac is founded

1650   1700   1750

1632 The Dutch settle New Amsterdam

1685 French explorer de La Salle builds a colony along the coast of present-day Texas

VOCABULARY

prehistory p. 9

artifact p. 9

resource p. 10

hunter-gatherer p. 11

technology p. 13

READING SKILL

Sequence Events
Copy the chart. As you read, fill it in with events from the lesson.

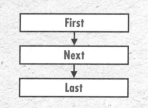

First
Next
Last

STANDARDS FOCUS

SOCIAL STUDIES People, Places, and Environments

GEOGRAPHY The Uses of Geography

THE FIRST AMERICANS

Cahokia was one of the first cities in North America.

Visual Preview

How did the first Americans use resources to survive?

A Early Americans built a city called Cahokia.

B The Eastern Woodlands people formed a union.

C The Pueblo and Lakota lived in the Southwest.

D Native Americans adapted to their environment.

A EARLY AMERICANS

*How did the first Americans get here? They probably walked for thousands of miles from Asia. Others may have come in small boats from Europe. They came long ago during the last Ice Age, a time called **prehistory**, before written history.*

To find out about our prehistory scientists called archaeologists use artifacts. Almost anything that people used long ago can be an artifact—tools, weapons, clothes, even jewelry. These earliest Americans used stone tools and weapons, hunted wild animals, and picked wild plants for food.

Cahokia

About the year 700, a group known as the Mississippians built a city near the Mississippi River, across from where St. Louis, Missouri, is now. The city, Cahokia, was one of the very first cities in North America. About 20,000 people lived there. How could so many people have enough to eat?

Unlike the earlier people who hunted and gathered their food, the Mississippians were farmers. They had learned to grow corn, and were able to grow enough to feed a large population. Since they were located at the center of trade routes that crisscrossed most of North America, they also became traders. Cahokia became a center for arts and crafts. Sometime around 1300, Cahokia was abandoned.

PEOPLE

MOUND BUILDERS

For about 3,000 years, the Adena, Hopewell, and Mississippian cultures lived in the Ohio and Mississippi River valleys. We call them mound builders because they built huge mounds of earth in their towns and cities. Some mounds were used as burial sites, while others had temples and homes built on top.

QUICK CHECK

Sequence When was Cahokia built?

B EASTERN WOODLANDS

Many years ago, the eastern half of North America was covered with forests. These forests were a good material, or **resource,** for the Native Americans that lived there.

Hunting and Farming

The people of the Eastern Woodlands got their food from the forest. They hunted deer and other animals.

AN IROQUOIS LONGHOUSE

smoke hole

storage platform

cooking

elm tree bark

sleeping platform

preparing animal skins

They also gathered fruits, nuts, and grains. People who get most of their food by hunting wild animals and gathering wild plants are known as **hunter-gatherers**.

Some people of the Eastern Woodlands, such as the Lenape, also grew their own food. Their most important crops were maize, beans, and squash.

A United People

Over time, some Native American groups decided to join forces with other groups. One of these united groups was the Iroquois.

The Iroquois people formed a union with five different Native American groups that set up a government called the Iroquois League. Each member had a say in how the government was run. Later, a sixth group joined.

The Iroquois League was very successful. It was so successful that some believe it influenced the founders of our own government.

QUICK CHECK
Summarize What was the Iroquois League?

gathering berries

collecting firewood

Diagram Skill

What jobs do you see people doing?

EVENT

TRAVELING WITH TEEPEES

The Plains people moved around a lot following the buffalo. They needed a home they could put up and take down easily. Teepees could do that. Teepees were made of wooden poles with buffalo hides stretched over them. Some had painted patterns on them that described hunts and battles or that told of the family's origins.

The Great Plains are a grassy, flat area in the middle of the United States. Near the Great Plains is a dry landscape known as the Southwest region. Native Americans in this region used the resources available to them.

The Lakota and Comanche

The Lakota lived in the northern part of the Great Plains. They were always moving, because the Lakota followed the buffalo. They used the buffalo for everything, including food, clothing, shelter, and tools.

The Comanche lived further south. It was warmer than the north, so grains and nuts were easier to find. Like the Lakota, the Comanche depended on the buffalo, but the Comanche also traded clothing and tools for fresh food with nearby farming peoples.

People of the Southwest

Long ago, a people known as the Ancestral Pueblo moved to the Southwest. They built towns high up in shallow caves along cliff walls. They left these communities around 1300. Their descendents, the

The Ancestral Pueblo built this community in the side of a cliff. It had 150 rooms and 23 kivas. A kiva is a common area used for ceremonies.

Pueblo people, built similar towns, and still live in the area today. The Spanish, the first Europeans to meet them, called these Native Americans Pueblo. Pueblo is the Spanish word for town or village.

The Pueblo and other Native Americans in the Southwest learned to farm in a hot, dry land. Their technology, or skills and tools, allowed them to grow corn and squash in the sandy soil. Others, such as the Apache, moved across the region, following buffalo and other large animals.

Quick Check

Why did the Lakota live in teepees?

Hidden under animal skins, hunters could creep close to a buffalo.

D THE WEST

PLACES

OZETTE

Ozette is an ancient Makah village in Washington state. It was buried by a mudslide around the year 1500. Since 1970, archaeologists have dug up more than 55,000 artifacts, including toys, baskets, hats, and tools from the site. Today, fishing hats are very similar to the fishing hats worn by Makah hundreds of years ago.

The western United States is a very large region. Today, eleven states are in the western region. Many different Native American groups lived in the West.

Native Americans of the West, like all people, learned to adapt to their surroundings. Each group's economy was influenced by the environment. This was true whether they lived in the mountains, along the coast, or in the desert.

The Northwest coast, from Oregon to Alaska, was a place rich in resources. People such as the Makah didn't have to farm. There were plenty of berries, roots, and other wild plants to gather. Sometimes they hunted beaver, bear, deer, and elk in the forest, but most of their food came from the sea. They fished and gathered seaweeds and shellfish.

Ozette was a busy Makah village in the 1400s.

A Region of Plenty

Like the Makah, the Tlingit went to the sea for food. They developed technology to build dams and traps for catching salmon. They also made large canoes that could travel long distances. They traded their surplus resources with neighboring people. This made the Tlingit wealthy.

Native Americans who lived in the mountains hunted and gathered food from the forests. Some, such as the Nez Perce, also fished in the mountain streams.

The West has a vast, dry region known as the Great Basin. People such as the Shoshone had to use the resources of the Great Basin carefully. These hunter-gatherers had to keep moving to find food.

Tlingit totem pole in Sitka National Historic Park in Alaska ▶

QUICK CHECK

Make Inferences How do the Makah use resources today?

Check Understanding

1. **VOCABULARY** Summarize this lesson using these vocabulary words.

   resource   technology

2. **READING SKILL   Sequence Events** Use the chart from page 8 to tell about Cahokia.

First
↓
Next
↓
Last

3. **Write About It** Why is it important to learn about the history of Native Americans?

EXPLORE The Big Idea

Lesson 2

VOCABULARY

mission p. 18

Northwest Passage p. 19

colony p. 19

READING SKILL

Sequence Events
Copy the chart. As you read, fill it in with events from the lesson.

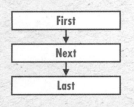

| First |
| Next |
| Last |

STANDARDS FOCUS

SOCIAL STUDIES — Global Connections

GEOGRAPHY — Places and Regions

THREE WORLDS MEET

The arrival of Columbus and his ships in the Caribbean changed the world forever.

Visual Preview

How did settlers in North America affect Native Americans?

A Columbus met Native Americans on a Caribbean Island.

B Spanish and French explorers settle in North America.

C English and Dutch settlers make colonies.

D The French and British fight over Native American lands.

16

THE FIRST EUROPEANS

In the middle 1400s, many Europeans read a book that told of jewels, delicious spices, and other wonders of China. Europeans wanted to get some of these amazing things.

At the time, the journey from Europe to Asia took a long time. A man named Christopher Columbus wanted to try a faster route. In 1492 he set out with three ships for Asia. Instead of sailing east, he sailed west. When he finally landed, he wasn't in Asia. He was on an island in the Caribbean Sea.

This was the beginning of an exchange that would forever change the lives of Europeans, Native Americans, and Africans. The Spanish introduced horses and oranges to Native Americans, while Europeans learned about chocolate, tomatoes, and popcorn.

The meeting wasn't always good. In time, Europeans took over the land. Native Americans had no immunity against European diseases, and huge numbers of Native Americans died. Many Africans were brought to the Americas against their wills.

EVENT

THE COLUMBIAN EXCHANGE

Suppose you had never eaten chocolate, potatoes, or corn! American foods were unknown in Europe until returning sailors brought them back. These foods eventually became a part of the European diet.

Native Americans await the arrival of European ships.

QUICK CHECK

Summarize How did the encounter between Europeans, Native Americans, and Africans change their lives forever?

17

B THE SPANISH AND FRENCH IN NORTH AMERICA

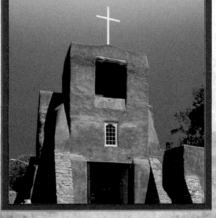

PLACES

SANTA FE

One of the earliest Spanish settlements was Santa Fe, now the capital of New Mexico. San Miguel Chapel in Santa Fe, built around 1610, is one of the oldest churches in the United States.

The first Europeans to explore North America were from Spain. A few were accompanied by African explorers. They thought they would find gold and other riches. Explorers such as Francisco Coronado traveled throughout the Southwest.

Priests also came to North America to talk about Christianity and settle the area. They set up **missions**, or settlements, throughout the West and Southwest. By the late 1600s, Spain controlled Mexico, much of South America, and most of what is now the southwestern United States and Florida.

Coronado traveled throughout the Southwest with a large expedition between 1540 and 1542.

French Traders

The French also explorered North America. They hoped to find a route that would lead from the Great Lakes to Asia. They called it the **Northwest Passage**. As it turned out, no such route existed, but the French explorers claimed these lands for France.

The French explorers were looking for gold and fur. At that time, hats and coats made of beaver fur were very fashionable in France. French trappers came and offered Native Americans weapons and metal tools in exchange for the plentiful beaver furs.

Soon, France claimed a huge piece of North America for itself and made it a **colony**—a land ruled by another country. They called it New France. Like the Spanish, the French also sent priests to teach Native Americans about Christianity.

QUICK CHECK

Summarize **Why did the French explore North America?**

PEOPLE

RENÉ-ROBERT CAVELIER, SIEUR DE LA SALLE

Robert de la Salle explored the Great Lakes region and the Mississippi River. In 1682 he traveled from present-day St. Louis to the Mississippi's mouth at the Gulf of Mexico. He named the area Louisiana in honor of the French king, Louis the Fourteenth.

C THE DUTCH AND ENGLISH IN NORTH AMERICA

The French and the Spanish weren't the only nations in Europe that wanted settlements in North America. The English and the Dutch also wanted colonies in North America. They wanted to find riches for their countries.

The English Colonies

In 1607, after a few failed attempts at settling in North America, a new group of English settlers set up a colony in what is now Virginia. They called the settlement Jamestown in honor of King James of England. The first Africans arrived in Jamestown in 1619. It became the first permanent English colony in North America and helped set a pattern for later colonists to follow.

New Amsterdam as it was in 1640

EVENT

THANKSGIVING

In 1620 people called Pilgrims left England in search of religious freedom. They landed in what is now part of New England and named their colony Plymouth. The Pilgrims survived with help from Native Americans. Pilgrims and Native Americans celebrated their friendship by having a great feast in the autumn of 1621. This feast has been called our country's first Thanksgiving.

New Netherland

The Dutch, like the French, came to North America to make money, particularly in the fur trade. They came from the Netherlands. In 1624 they settled along the Hudson River and named their colony New Netherland.

Two years later, the Dutch governor, Peter Minuit, bought Manhattan Island from Native Americans living there and called it New Amsterdam.

The English colonies began to spread out, and in 1664 they took control of New Amsterdam from the Dutch. New Amsterdam soon changed its name to New York. The English also began colonizing other lands near the Atlantic coast. By 1732 England had thirteen colonies stretching from New Hampshire to Georgia.

QUICK CHECK

Sequence Events What happened in New Netherland after the Dutch settled there?

PEOPLE

POCAHONTAS

Pocahontas was the daughter of Powhatan, a Native American leader who lived near Jamestown. She became a link between Jamestown settlers and her own people.

Land was what everyone wanted in the 1700s. The English, French, Dutch, and the Spanish kept coming to North America. This was hard for the Native Americans who had been living there because all these new colonists wanted more land.

Native Americans look over an English fort.

The French and Indian War

The French and the English, who had been enemies in Europe, started fighting in North America, too. When the English colonies began filling up, English settlers started to head west into the Great Lakes region and the Ohio River valley. These lands had already been claimed by France. Before long, the English and the French were at war over the question of who owned the land.

Many Native Americans in the region fought alongside the French in this war. They hoped that the French could help them drive the English out of North America altogether. For this reason, the war was called the French and Indian War.

British Victory

Even though the French had help from Native Americans, the English won the war in 1763. The English seized the Ohio River valley. Great Britain now claimed almost all of the present-day United States east of the Mississippi River. To the surprise of the Native Americans, they chose to keep English settlers out of the Ohio River valley and leave the land to the Native Americans.

QUICK CHECK

Summarize What sparked the French and Indian War?

PEOPLE

GEORGE WASHINGTON

In 1753 George Washington delivered a letter to the French army, demanding they leave the Ohio territory. The French refused. A year later, Washington's troops ambushed a French Canadian scouting party. This was the beginning of the French and Indian War.

Check Understanding

1. **VOCABULARY** Draw a picture to illustrate each word below. Label each picture.

    mission   colony

2. **READING SKILL Sequence Events** Use the chart from page 16 to describe French explorers in North America.

First
Next
Last

3. **Write About It** How were some Native Americans treated by the new settlers? Give examples.

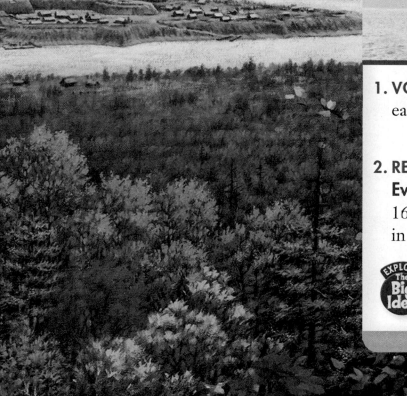

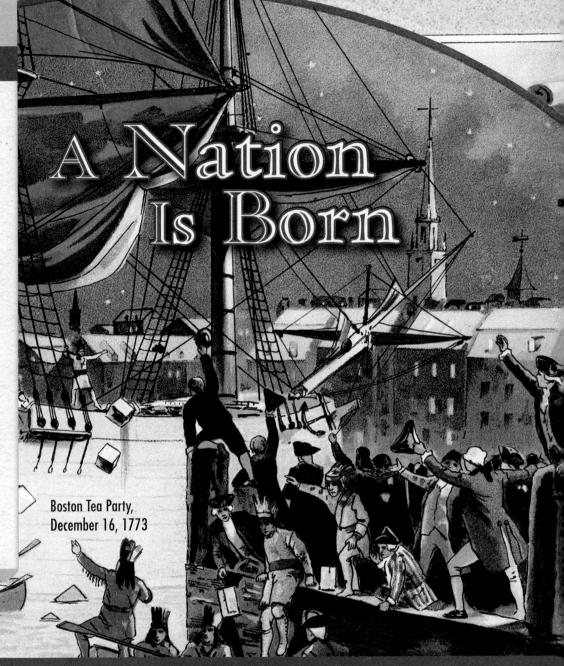

Lesson 3

VOCABULARY

tax p. 25

revolution p. 25

Declaration of Independence p. 27

independent p. 30

READING SKILL

Sequence Events
Copy the chart. Fill it in with events from the lesson.

First
↓
Next
↓
Last

STANDARDS FOCUS

SOCIAL STUDIES — Civic Ideals and Practices

GEOGRAPHY — Human Systems

A Nation Is Born

Boston Tea Party,
December 16, 1773

Visual Preview

Why was independence important to the colonists?

A Great Britain taxed colonists. The colonists protested.

B The colonists prepared for war and independence.

C Great Britain and Patriot soldiers went to war.

D The colonies became an independent nation.

A TAXES AND PROTESTS

*The French and Indian War was expensive. Great Britain needed a way to pay for it. They decided to make the colonists pay new **taxes**. Taxes are money paid to a government for its support.*

Many of the colonists were already angry because Great Britain had said they couldn't settle west of the Appalachian Mountains. Settlers wanted those lands. When Great Britain's lawmakers (called Parliament) made them pay taxes, they got even angrier. They said Great Britain was being unfair. The colonists were also upset that they didn't have any representatives in Parliament to vote. The people in Great Britain did. Some colonists thought about having a **revolution** to break from the government, but most colonists didn't want that at the time. All they wanted was the same rights as people in Great Britain.

When the government passed a tax on tea, the colonists were angrier than ever. First, they refused to buy the tea. Then, they decided to show Great Britain exactly what they thought of the tax. One night, a group of men sneaked on board three British ships in Boston Harbor and dumped a load of expensive tea overboard. The event, known as the Boston Tea Party, made the British government furious.

QUICK CHECK

Sequence Events Which came first, the Stamp Act or the tax on tea?

THE ROAD TO WAR

PLACES

INDEPENDENCE HALL

In 1776, representatives from the 13 colonies met in this Philadelphia building to sign the Declaration of Independence. Later they would meet here to approve the United States Constitution. "Independence Hall" is now a museum.

Great Britain wanted to punish the colonists for dumping the tea. It forbade the colonists to hold town meetings and closed the harbor until the colonists paid for the tea they had dumped. Colonists couldn't pay for the tea if the harbor was closed—that's where half of the people in Boston worked. This made the colonists angrier. People began to worry that they might starve. By the spring of 1775, things were very tense in Boston. The colonists finally felt the situation had gone on long enough. They were going to do something about their problem. More people began talking about independence.

The British government sent soldiers to Boston and said that it was to "protect" the colonists, but Britain wanted to show the colonists that it had control.

Battle of Lexington, 1775

The First Shots

In April 1775, British spies learned that colonists were storing weapons in nearby Concord. Soldiers started to march from Boston to Concord to seize the weapons. A colonist named Paul Revere heard about their plan and rode toward Concord to warn the town. "The British are coming!" he called out all along the way.

The next morning, volunteer soldiers were waiting when the British troops reached Lexington. Fighting broke out in Lexington and again at Concord. The American Revolution had begun.

Declaring Freedom

In the summer of 1776, a group of colonists met and chose Thomas Jefferson to write the **Declaration of Independence**. It told the world why the colonies wanted independence. Signing this document took courage. It also meant war.

QUICK CHECK

Main Idea and Details How did the British respond to the Boston Tea Party?

PEOPLE

Crispus Attucks

Crispus Attucks, a person who had escaped from slavery, was one of five people killed by British soldiers during the Boston Massacre in 1770.

C FIGHTING THE WAR

Strengths and Weaknesses

At the beginning of the war, all of Europe, and a good many Americans, didn't think the colonists stood a chance against Great Britain. The British navy was the best in the world. Its army had huge supplies of guns and ammunition. Many Patriot soldiers didn't have uniforms. Guns and food were in short supply. The Patriots had some advantages. They were defending their homes and knew the land well.

Since Great Britain was very far away, it was expensive to send supplies and troops across the Atlantic to fight in North America. People in Great Britain began to wonder whether the war was worth the trouble.

PEOPLE

DEBORAH SAMPSON

Deborah Sampson was a Massachusetts woman. She so strongly believed in the Patriot cause that she disguised herself as a man and joined the army. At that time, women were not allowed to fight in wars. She served for nearly a year before she was struck by a fever and her secret was discovered.

British Soldiers

Native Americans and African Americans

At first, Native Americans refused to take sides. Later, the British convinced some of the Iroquois Confederacy to help them. The Iroquois were angry that the settlers had taken their lands. They believed that if Great Britain won, the colonies would not expand into their homelands. About 5,000 African Americans served as soldiers in the Continental Army. Others piloted boats and worked as shipyard carpenters in the Patriot Navy.

QUICK CHECK

Summarize What advantages and disadvantages did the Patriots have in the war with England?

PLACES

VALLEY FORGE

George Washington and his army spent the winter of 1777–1778 in Valley Forge, Pennsylvania. About 2,500 patriots died of hunger, cold, and disease during the long, cold winter. Today you can visit the Valley Forge National Historic Park.

Patriot Soldiers

Patriots were able to hold off British soldiers even though they lacked training and supplies.

JAMES MADISON

We can thank James Madison for our Constitution. It was Madison who planned it, wrote it, and fought for its approval. He is known today as "the father of the Constitution."

Despite all the odds, and without any help, the Patriots held on. Finally, France decided to give the Patriots a hand against its old enemy. France sent soldiers and supplies to help the Patriots. Later, Spain decided to give a hand, too. At last, in 1781, the British surrendered at Yorktown, Virginia. What had once been thirteen colonies were now an **independent** nation, the United States of America. This meant they were no longer governed by Great Britain. The new nation stretched from the Atlantic Ocean to the Mississippi River.

Constitutional Convention, Philadelphia

A Plan for Government

The next task was to plan a new government. The country struggled for ten years, but it was soon clear that the plan the patriots had for a new government did not work. In 1787 leaders came together and agreed on a different plan of government—a new constitution. The United States Constitution divided power between the states and the national government. The Constitution was approved by the states in 1788. Three years later, the Bill of Rights was added. The Constitution is still the law of our country today.

QUICK CHECK

Summarize How did the French and Spanish help the Patriots to become an independent nation?

Check Understanding

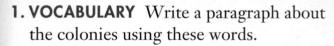

1. **VOCABULARY** Write a paragraph about the colonies using these words.

   tax   revolution   independent

2. **READING SKILL Sequence Events** Use the chart from page 24 to tell what led to war.

First
Next
Last

3. **Write About It** How did the patriots form their own nation?

VOCABULARY

territory p. 33

Louisiana Purchase p. 34

expedition p. 34

canal p. 36

frontier p. 38

READING SKILL

Sequence Events
Copy the chart. As you read, fill it in with information about the growth of our nation.

First
↓
Next
↓
Last

STANDARDS FOCUS

SOCIAL STUDIES Time, Continuity, and Change

GEOGRAPHY Environment and Society

THE NATION GROWS

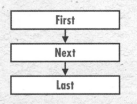

A farmer plows

Visual Preview

What were the effects of growth on the new nation?

A The Northwest Territory caused conflict.

B Lewis and Clark explored lands of the Louisiana Purchase.

C Canals and railroads made travel faster.

D Texas freedom and gold helped the country grow.

Ⓐ OVER THE MOUNTAINS

Great Britain had closed the land west of the Appalachians to settlers. Now that the country was independent, some settlers began moving west. They were looking for inexpensive land and good soil.

The new United States government passed two laws to oversee the vast new territory west of the mountains. The first law called for the land to be measured. The second law officially named the area north of the Ohio River as the Northwest **Territory**. A territory is land owned by a country. The law also stated that once enough settlers lived there, the territory could become a state. Slavery was not allowed in the territory or states.

Growth and Conflict

Congress thought Native Americans would be willing to sell their land. Many were angry that the treaties they had signed with the British meant little to the settlers. Several Native American nations attacked the settlers. After they lost the Battle of Fallen Timbers in Ohio, many Native American leaders had to sign a treaty giving up their lands.

In 1800 part of the Northwest Territory had enough people to become the territory of Ohio. A year later, the western part of the Northwest Territory became the territory of Indiana.

PEOPLE

TECUMSEH

Tecumseh was a Shawnee chief. He traveled great distances visiting Native American villages. He tried to get them to unite to protect their lands. Despite his leadership, Native Americans were forced to give up most of their land in the Northwest Territory.

QUICK CHECK

Sequence What happened after Native Americans refused to sell their land?

Ⓑ MOVING WEST

By 1803, the United States controlled most of the land east of the Mississippi River. Still, many Americans were eager to push past the Mississippi River into Louisiana Territory. At the time, Louisiana belonged to France.

France needed money for a war it was fighting in Europe against Great Britain. The French offered to sell all of Louisiana to President Thomas Jefferson. Jefferson agreed and bought the entire territory for about $15 million. The new territory, known as the **Louisiana Purchase**, was huge. It stretched from the Mississippi River to the Rocky Mountains. Americans knew little about this area.

Lewis and Clark

Jefferson wanted to know everything about the land he had just bought. He organized an **expedition**, or a journey of exploration. He hired Meriwether Lewis and William Clark to lead it. He asked them to make maps as they traveled and to record what they found.

Lewis and Clark traveled on the Missouri River for much of their journey.

PEOPLE

SACAGAWEA

Sacagawea helped Lewis and Clark speak with the Native Americans they met. She also showed them which plants were safe to eat. Sacagawea's brother, a Shoshone chief, provided the group with horses to continue the journey over the mountains.

Lewis and Clark hired a French trader named Charbonneau and his Shoshone wife, Sacagawea, as guides. For two years, they led more than 40 men across the West. They climbed high mountains in terrible weather.

The expedition reached the Pacific Ocean in 1805. By 1806, they had returned to Missouri. They brought back exciting information about America's new territory.

QUICK CHECK

Cause and Effect Why did Jefferson send Lewis and Clark into Louisiana?

When they could, Lewis and Clark traveled by boat. ▶

As more and more people came, the **frontier**, or the edge of the settled area, kept moving west. Some Americans began to feel that the United States had a right to all of the land out west—that it was the country's destiny to extend from the Atlantic to the Pacific.

Texas and the Mexican War

Mexico won its independence from Spain in 1821. Americans began settling in northern Mexico in the 1820s in an area named Texas. They soon outnumbered the Mexicans living there. Then, in 1835, some of the Americans started a revolution. Americans living in Texas wanted to be independent from Mexico. In April 1836, they defeated the Mexican Army and won their independence. The government of the new nation asked to join the United States. In 1845 the United States government agreed, and Texas became the 28th state.

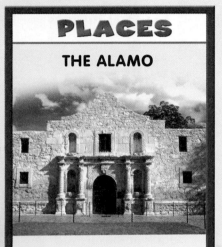

PLACES

THE ALAMO

The Alamo was a mission in San Antonio, Texas, that later became a fort. In 1836 it was the site of a bloody battle between Texas settlers and the Mexican army. Among the settlers who defended the Alamo were Sam Houston and Davy Crockett. Today, the Alamo is a museum.

Settlers in wagon trains traveled across the Nebraska plains.

Mexico and the United States disagreed about where the border of Texas should be. The United States and Mexico went to war over this in 1846. The United States won. In the peace treaty of 1848, Mexico gave up half its territory, including California. In return, the United States paid Mexico $15 million.

The California Gold Rush

In 1848 a California settler discovered gold. The news spread rapidly across the country. Thousands of people traveled to California. They hoped to become rich. Two years after gold was first discovered, California had enough people for statehood.

▲ Thousands of people looked for gold in California.

QUICK CHECK

Cause and Effect How did the United States expand westward?

Check Understanding

1. **VOCABULARY** Write a sentence for each of the following vocabulary words.

   canal   frontier   territory

2. **READING SKILL Sequence Events** Use the chart from page 32 to describe movement westward.

   | First |
   | Next |
   | Last |

3. **Write About It** How did the growth of the United States bring people into conflict?

EXPLORE The Big Idea

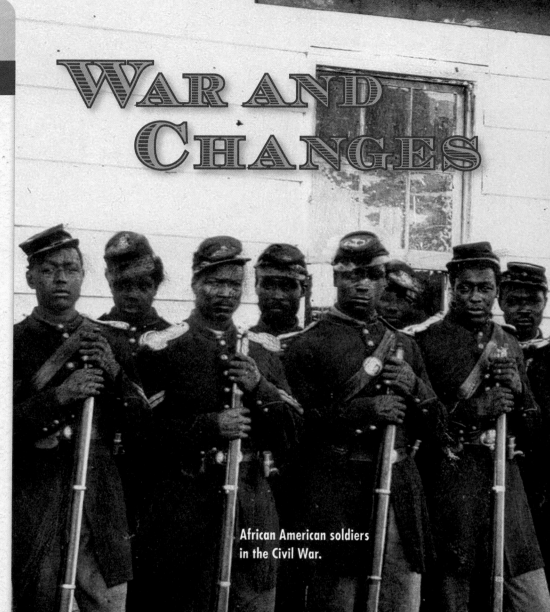

Lesson 5

READING SKILL

Sequence Events
Copy the chart. As you read, fill it in with information about the Civil War.

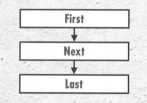

First
↓
Next
↓
Last

STANDARDS FOCUS

SOCIAL STUDIES Individuals, Groups, and Institutions

GEOGRAPHY Places and Regions

WAR AND CHANGES

African American soldiers in the Civil War.

Visual Preview

How did the Civil War change the nation?

A The North has industry. The Civil War begins.

B Lincoln issues the Emancipation Proclamation.

C Reconstruction begins and the nation is rebuilt.

D Immigrants move to the plains and ideas bring progress.

Ⓐ NORTH AND SOUTH

By 1850, differences between the North and the South were threatening to split the country. As each new territory became a state, people in the North and South argued about whether slavery would be allowed there.

In the South, a way of life had come to depend on slave labor. In the North, slavery had been abolished, or made illegal, by this time. Many Northerners worked in factories and were paid wages. They saw slavery as a threat to wage labor. Others saw it as a terrible moral wrong. Some people in the North began to oppose slavery.

The Nation Divides

Then came the election of 1860. Abraham Lincoln, who was against the spread of slavery, was elected President. Many Southerners were afraid that Lincoln wanted to end slavery altogether. One by one, in the early months of 1861, Southern states broke away from the United States. They formed the Confederate States of America, with Jefferson Davis as their President.

In April 1861, Confederate forces opened fire on Fort Sumter. The **Civil War**, or the war between the Union and the Confederacy, had begun.

PEOPLE

HARRIET BEECHER STOWE

In 1852 Harriet Beecher Stowe published *Uncle Tom's Cabin*, a novel about enslaved men and women. Stowe's book described the evils of slavery. More and more people wanted to end slavery because of this book.

In the North, people worked in factories making goods such as cloth. ▼

QUICK CHECK

Sequence What did Southern states do after Lincoln was elected in 1860?

STRENGTHS AND WEAKNESSES

Both sides had strengths and weaknesses. The South's greatest strength was its army. Men in the South knew how to ride horses and hunt, which were good skills for soldiers. The South also had many well-trained officers. Robert E. Lee, one of these officers, became the commander of the Confederate army. However, one of the South's weaknesses was that the farms there grew mostly cotton, not food.

EVENT

THE *MONITOR* AND THE *VIRGINIA*

During the 1860s, most warships were made of wood. The Union ship *Monitor* and the Confederate ship *Virginia*, however, were ironclads. Their iron sides protected them from cannonballs and made them hard to sink. In an 1862 battle, neither ship could sink the other.

Union and Confederacy

Union state
Confederate state
Territory
— Boundary between United States and Confederate States

PACIFIC OCEAN

ATLANTIC OCEAN

OR
MN
WI
MI
NY
VT
ME
NH
MA
RI
CT
NJ
DE
MD
IA
PA
CA
IL
IN
OH
KS
MO
WV
VA
KY
TN
NC
AR
SC
MS
AL
GA
TX
LA
FL

0   200   400 miles
0   200 400 kilometers

The North had a much larger population than the Confederacy, but the people did not have many fighting skills. The North had supplies for a larger army because most of the country's factories were there. The factories made weapons and uniforms. The North also grew most of the country's food. Plus, the North had most of the railroads that could move troops and supplies.

Lincoln Ends Slavery

At first, Lincoln wanted to keep the Union together. Soon, the goal of the war included ending slavery. On January 1, 1863, Lincoln issued the **Emancipation Proclamation**. This document said that all enslaved people in the Confederacy "shall be . . . forever free."

More than 600,000 men from the Union and the Confederacy died during the war. Finally, on April 9, 1865, after four years of fighting, the Confederacy surrendered. Northerners celebrated at first, but joy quickly turned to sadness. On April 14, 1865, President Lincoln was shot and killed as he watched a play in Washington, D.C.

PEOPLE

ABRAHAM LINCOLN
In 1865, near the end of the War, Lincoln spoke about healing the nation. His wish was to bring the country together "with malice towards none, with charity for all."

In 1863 the Union army won a major victory at Gettysburg, Pennsylvania. ▼

QUICK CHECK

Summary What were the strengths and weaknesses of the two sides that fought in the Civil War?

C REBUILDING THE NATION

Now came the job of putting the nation back together again. This period became known as **Reconstruction**. President Johnson's plan for rebuilding the country was to have the Southern states pledge their loyalty to the Union and abolish slavery. By the fall of 1865, every state but Texas had rejoined the Union.

Important Changes

Congress also amended, or changed, the Constitution. The changes were written in the 13th, 14th, and 15th amendments to the Constitution. They made slavery illegal, said that all people born in the United States were citizens, gave all male citizens the right to vote, and protected the rights of all citizens.

Violence and Jim Crow Laws

Most white Southerners did not want African Americans to be treated as their equals. The new parts of the Constitution were often not enforced, and African Americans were denied their rights. Laws called Jim Crow laws were passed to make the separation of African Americans and whites legal. People who tried to object were threatened and sometimes killed.

After emancipation, thousands of African Americans tried to find their families. Many were reunited, but others were not. Some former slaves moved out of the South, hoping to find a better life. Many stayed where they were.

QUICK CHECK

Main Idea and Details What changes did Congress make to the Constitution after the Civil War?

PUBLISHED & PRINTED BY

1 *Reading Emancipation Proclama*
2 *Life Liberty and Independence*
3 *We Unite the Bonds of Fellowship*
4 *Our Charter of Rights the Holy Scr*

This poster shows people and events related to the passing of the 15th Amendment to the Constitution, which gave the right to vote to all male citizens.

D NEW SETTLERS, NEW TECHNOLOGIES

After the Civil War, pioneers began moving westward to claim cheap land on the Great Plains. Many of the **immigrants**, who came to the United States from places as far away as Germany, Norway, and Russia, also headed west. An immigrant is a person who comes to a new country to live. The population of the United States grew.

The Plains Wars

What about the Native Americans that already lived on the Great Plains? They were losing more and more land to settlers. In addition, white hunters were wiping out the buffalo, destroying the Native Americans' way of life.

The Lakota, Cheyenne, and Arapaho joined together to protect their lands. They fought United States soldiers at battles such as Little Bighorn, but in the end, they lost. By 1877, the last Native Americans of the Great Plains were moved to reservations.

PEOPLE

THOMAS EDISON

Edison invented many things we now take for granted. In 1879 he perfected the first practical light bulb. A few years later, he developed a system that made it possible to provide electricity to an entire city.

As trains made travel easier, people began to build small towns where they stopped.

PUBLIC SCHOOL

Technology Changes Lives

Meanwhile, dozens of **inventions**, or new products, were changing American lives. Farmers had new machinery that made work easier. The telephone was invented in 1876 by Alexander Graham Bell. Telephones made it easier for Americans to communicate. Electric lights made it easier and safer for people to work indoors and at night. A cheaper way was found to make steel, and soon, steel was used to build skyscrapers and improve railroad tracks.

With machinery to do the work, farms needed fewer workers. Many people found jobs in factories that were built to meet the demand for new goods. Immigrants continued to travel to "the land of opportunity." Many settled in the growing cities.

QUICK CHECK

Draw Conclusions How did telephones change life in America?

Check Understanding

1. **VOCABULARY** Write a paragraph about the end of the war using these words.

   Reconstruction   immigrant

2. **READING SKILL Sequence Events** Use the chart on page 40 to tell about slavery ending.

   First
   ↓
   Next
   ↓
   Last

3. **Write About It** What events helped to shape the nation in the late 1800s?

Lesson 6

VOCABULARY

suffrage p. 51

dictator p. 55

Allies p. 55

Axis p. 55

READING SKILL

Sequence Events
Copy the chart. As you read, fill it in with information about World War I, the Great Depression, and World War II.

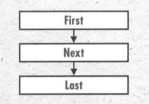

First
↓
Next
↓
Last

STANDARDS FOCUS

SOCIAL STUDIES Time, Continuity, and Change

GEOGRAPHY Human Systems

This home in San Simeon, California, stood in sharp contrast to the homes of those who lived in poverty.

Visual Preview

How did economic and political changes affect the nation?

A There was a sharp contrast between the wealthy and poor.

B Changes came about with World War I and women's suffrage.

C The Great Depression took place at the end of the 1920s.

D The New Deal helped America after World War II.

A   A TIME OF CONTRASTS

In the early part of the 20th century, there were some big differences in the way people lived in our country. People such as Cornelius Vanderbilt, John D. Rockefeller, and Andrew Carnegie were millionaires. At the same time, many people lived in terrible poverty, especially in the cities.

Although there were some millionaires in the United States, most people worked ten hours or more a day, sometimes as many as 80 hours a week. They worked in factories that were hot, crowded, and often dangerous. Even children as young as five or six worked in mines and factories. If workers complained, they were fired.

Working for Change

Wealthy people such as Carnegie and Rockefeller gave money to help people. Others also tried to improve life for the poor. Jane Addams opened a house in Chicago where poor people could get an education and advice.

Workers began to join together to form labor unions. Unions are groups of workers who organize to make agreements with employers about better wages and safer working conditions.

PLACES

THE STATUE OF LIBERTY

The Statue of Liberty stands on an island in New York Harbor. France gave the statue to the United States as a gift in 1886. To many immigrants, the statue symbolized justice and freedom.

QUICK CHECK

Sequence What did workers do to get safer working conditions?

In cities, children played in alleys. ▶

Ⓑ A TIME OF CONFLICT

In 1914 a struggle for power in Europe led to war. England, France, Japan, Italy, and Russia were the Allied Powers. They were fighting Germany, Austria-Hungary, and Turkey, or the Central Powers. So many countries were involved in this struggle that people called it the "Great War." Later, it became known as World War I.

At first, the United States tried to stay out of the war. After all, the battles were happening in Europe. Finally, in 1917, the United States joined the side of the Allied Powers. The United States helped win the war against the Central Powers.

As the United States entered World War I, posters such as this one encouraged citizens to join the armed forces. ▼

follow the Boys in Blue for Home and Country

ENLIST IN THE NAVY

Changes for Women

Did you know that when the Constitution was written, only men could vote? As far back as the 1840s, some people were working for women's **suffrage**, or right to vote. In 1920 Congress finally amended the Constitution to give women the right to vote.

QUICK CHECK

Summarize What were some of the events of the early 1900s?

▼ These young girls hold signs to show that they want to vote when they are women.

C LIFE IN THE 1920s

After World War I ended, people wanted to forget their troubles. For many, the 1920s were good times. Many Americans had jobs and money to spend. Now that Henry Ford had found a cheaper way to build cars, it seemed almost everyone in America could buy one. Americans played phonograph records, listened to the radio, and went to the new moving picture shows.

Stocks

In the 1920s, many people bought stocks, or shares of businesses. People buy and sell their stock on the stock market. Buyers were hoping the stocks would go up in value and make them rich.

Prices had been going up and up, but then they started to fall. On October 29, 1929, stock owners panicked and rushed to sell their stocks all at once. The prices fell very quickly, or "crashed." The stock market crash put an end to the good times of the 1920s. Banks ran out of money and closed. Many businesses closed. Many people lost all their savings, and suddenly millions were out of work.

EVENT

THE OKIES

In the 1930s, many farmers fled the Dust Bowl. They came from many states, but most came from Oklahoma. Eventually, all of the migrants, no matter where they were from, became known as "Okies."

The Bad Times

The stock market crash began a period of economic hard times known as the Great Depression. People all over the country were out of work. People stood in bread and soup lines to get food. Some people sold apples or pencils on street corners.

Farmers had an especially hard time. Many farmers had borrowed money from banks to buy equipment. When the farmers could not pay back the loans, they lost their farms.

To make matters worse, many states were hit by a drought. The drought lasted for so long, the soil turned to dust and was blown around in dust storms. Texas, Oklahoma, and Kansas were the hardest-hit states. These areas became known as the Dust Bowl. Many Dust Bowl farmers moved to California, hoping for a better life.

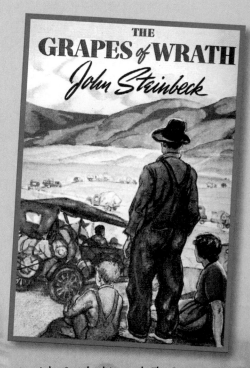

▲ John Steinbeck's novel, *The Grapes of Wrath*, tells the story of Dust Bowl farmers who left their homes for a chance at a better life in California.

QUICK CHECK

Cause and Effect What happened after stock prices crashed on October 29, 1929?

During the Great Depression, people stood in long lines to get food.

53

D RECOVERY AND WAR

In 1932 Franklin Roosevelt was elected President. In his first speech he declared,

"The only thing we have to fear is fear itself."

People were taking all their money out of banks because they were worried that the banks would close and their money would be gone. To stop people from doing this, Roosevelt declared a bank holiday and closed the banks.

A New Deal

The New Deal was a plan to help Americans recover from the Great Depression. Social Security was established to provide income to retired Americans. Other programs paid for building new roads and bringing electricity to rural areas. These projects created jobs and improved the quality of life for many people.

This World War II poster shows Franklin Roosevelt on the left and Winston Churchill on the right. ▼

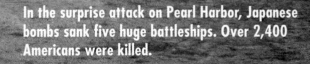

In the surprise attack on Pearl Harbor, Japanese bombs sank five huge battleships. Over 2,400 Americans were killed.

Another World War

Problems from World War I were still brewing in Europe. Adolf Hitler came to power in Germany in 1933. He was a **dictator**, or a person who rules a country without sharing power. In 1939 another world war began. The **Allies** were countries that fought against the **Axis** in World War II.

The Allies were England, France, and the Soviet Union. The Axis were Germany, Italy, and Japan. In 1941 Japan bombed the American naval base at Pearl Harbor, Hawaii, in a surprise attack. The United States joined the war on the side of the Allies.

Suddenly, the Great Depression was over. The war created new jobs and work for many Americans. Women worked in factories building tanks and airplanes. African Americans from the South moved north to work in cities. The Allies won World War II in 1945.

PEOPLE

WOMEN IN WWII

During World War II, so many men were away from home fighting the war that women were able to get jobs they had never had before. By the end of 1943, more than 300,000 women worked in the aircraft industry alone. Women also worked in the military in noncombat roles.

QUICK CHECK

Main Idea and Details **What ended the Great Depression?**

Check Understanding

1. **VOCABULARY** Create a poster about World War II using these words.

   dictator   Axis   Allies

2. **READING SKILL Sequence Events** Use the chart on page 48 to describe the events in the 1920s.

   | First |
   | Next |
   | Last |

3. **Write About It** How did the Great Depression affect the nation?

EXPLORE The Big Idea

Lesson 7

VOCABULARY

communism p. 57

discrimination p. 58

civil rights p. 58

terrorism p. 60

READING SKILL

Sequence Events
Copy the chart. As you read, fill it in with information about the modern United States.

First
↓
Next
↓
Last

STANDARDS FOCUS

SOCIAL STUDIES Individual Development and Identity

GEOGRAPHY Environment and Society

A MODERN WORLD

In the 1950s, cars became more important as many Americans moved to suburban communities such as this one in Levittown, New York.

Visual Preview

How did modern conflicts shape the country?

A The Cold War led to a space race.

B The civil rights movement worked for equal rights.

C America faces challenges and energy concerns.

Ⓐ A COLD WAR

In the late 20th century, we sent people to the moon and entered the computer age. It was a time of conflict, but also one of accomplishments and changes. Americans entered the 21st century ready to face the challenges ahead.

The Soviet Union, a group of nations controlled by Russia, fought on the same side as the Allies in World War II. The Soviet Union had a communist government—this meant that the government owned and controlled everything. After World War II, the United States began to worry that **communism** would spread. The two nations became enemies in the Cold War. The war was not fought with guns and armies, but instead with ideas and money.

The two nations were involved in an arms race. Each nation worked to build more atomic weapons than the other. Each side thought these powerful weapons would keep the other side from attacking.

A War in Korea

The Korean peninsula had been divided into two countries, North Korea and South Korea. North Korea had a communist government. In June 1950, North Korea attacked South Korea. The United States rushed troops to help South Korea. In 1953 a settlement was reached that ended the conflict between the two nations.

PEOPLE

HARRY S. TRUMAN

Harry S. Truman became President after the death of President Roosevelt. Truman's decision to use atomic bombs against Japan helped end World War II. Truman was also President during the Korean War.

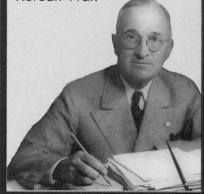

QUICK CHECK

Sequence Events When did the United States enter into a Cold War with the Soviet Union?

STRUGGLES AT HOME AND OVERSEAS

You might have thought that the Civil War improved the lives of African Americans. People of color were still not treated equally in many ways. In both the North and South, there was still **discrimination**, or an unfair difference in the way people are treated.

During World War II, African American soldiers and sailors had risked their lives just as other soldiers had. Now, they and others began demanding equal rights at home.

People joined together to take action. They began a **civil rights** movement. Civil rights are the rights of all citizens to be treated equally under the law. Leaders such as Martin Luther King, Jr., organized marches and protests to gather

In August 1963, thousands of people came to see Martin Luther King, Jr., speak about civil rights on the Mall in Washington, D.C.

support. In 1964 the first of several laws, called the Civil Rights Acts, were passed. Finally, discrimination was illegal.

Another War in Asia

Starting in 1961, the United States became involved in a war in Vietnam, a country in Southeast Asia. Americans were bitterly divided about the Vietnam War. Finally, in 1975, the United States brought its soldiers home.

QUICK CHECK

Sequence **Events** What happened before the Civil Rights Acts were passed?

THE SPACE RACE

During the 1960s, the Soviet Union and the United States competed not only on the ground, but also in space. Each country sent rockets and astronauts to explore space. In 1969 American astronaut Neil Armstrong became the first person to walk on the moon.

NEW CHALLENGES

EVENT

THE TECHNOLOGY EXPLOSION

When computers were first invented in the 1950s, one filled a whole room! In 1977 a desktop computer was invented. By 2003 two out of three Americans had computers in their homes. Today computers have changed the way people communicate.

On September 11, 2001, something happened that most Americans will never forget. Terrorists took over American airplanes and used them to attack the United States. Thousands of people died. President George W. Bush declared a war on **terrorism**. Terrorism, or using fear and violence to achieve political goals, has been a growing problem in the world.

President Bush created a new department called the Department of Homeland Security. One of the actions this department has taken is to increase the security at our airports. American troops were also sent to fight in Afghanistan and in Iraq, two countries in Asia whose leaders were believed to help terrorists.

▲ Windmills turn wind into energy that can be used to provide electricity to homes and businesses.

▲ Firefighters work to clear the rubble of the World Trade Center after the terrorist attacks of September 11, 2001.

New Kinds of Energy

Another huge challenge our nation faces is finding enough energy sources. Think about how our lives would be different if we ran out of gasoline for our cars or couldn't use electricity in our homes.

You know that gasoline is made from oil. The United States produces some oil, but not enough for everyone. We buy oil from other countries, including countries in the Middle East.

In August 2005, Hurricane Katrina hit the Gulf Coast of the United States. Our oil production in that region was completely shut down for a time. This event showed us how important it is to conserve energy and to find other types of fuel.

QUICK CHECK

Summarize What are some of the challenges facing the United States today?

EVENT

EARTH DAY

Burning gasoline produces carbon dioxide that can pollute the air. Since trees use carbon dioxide for food, one way people celebrate Earth Day is by planting trees to reduce air pollution. People also reduce how much energy and water they use.

Check Understanding

1. **VOCABULARY** Write a sentence for each vocabulary word.

   discrimination   terrorism   civil rights

2. **READING SKILL Sequence Events** Use the chart on page 56 to talk about the Cold War.

   First
   ↓
   Next
   ↓
   Last

3. 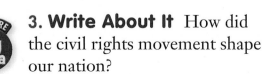 **Write About It** How did the civil rights movement shape our nation?

EXPLORE The Big Idea

Vocabulary Review

Copy the sentences below. Use the list of vocabulary words to fill in the blanks.

artifact   Louisiana Purchase

Civil War   terrorism

1. A(n) _____ can tell us about people of the past.

2. The territory that President Thomas Jefferson bought from the French was the _____.

3. The Union and Confederate armies fought in the _____ .

4. On September 11, 2001, an act of _____ occurred.

Comprehension and Critical Thinking

5. Why did colonists object to taxes passed by the British government?

6. Why was the transcontinental railroad important?

7. **Reading Skill** What events led to Sacagawea helping the Lewis and Clark expedition?

8. **Critical Thinking** What do you think was the most important invention of the 1800s?

Skill

Use Time Lines

Use the time line to answer each question.

9. Was gold discovered in California before or after Columbus's first visit to America?

10. How many years after Cahokia was built was gold discovered in California?

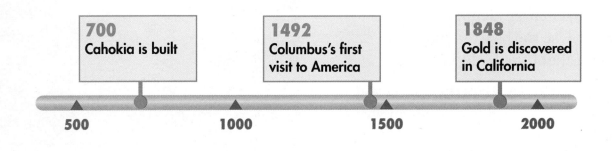

700	1492	1848
Cahokia is built	Columbus's first visit to America	Gold is discovered in California

500   1000   1500   2000

Test Preparation

Read the passage. Then answer the questions.

> The Huron were a Native American group that lived in what is now Michigan. The Huron way of life was built on family relationships. Among the Huron, children were members of their mother's clan, not their father's. When a man married, he became part of his wife's clan and went to live in her family's house.
>
> The Huron were loving parents. They believed that children learned from example, not from punishment. Huron children knew their parents would be disappointed if they misbehaved. The children did not want to let their families down, so they learned to do the right thing.

1. What is the main idea of this passage?

A. The Huron lived in Michigan.

B. Family relationships were important to the Huron.

C. The Huron punished their children.

D. The Huron had small families.

2. What inferences can be made from this passage?

A. Parents did not care for their children.

B. Huron children lived with their mothers only.

C. The children pleased their parents.

D. The Huron believed in discipline.

3. Which statement is an opinion?

A. The Huron were a Native American group.

B. Huron children did not want to let their families down.

C. Huron homes were very comfortable.

D. When a Huron man married he became a part of his wife's clan.

4. How might the Huron have come to the conclusion that children learn best by example?

The Big Idea Activities

What are some events that have shaped our nation?

Write About the Big Idea

FOLDABLES™
Study Organizer

Narrative Essay

In Unit 1 you read about some of the events that have shaped our nation. Review your notes in the completed foldable. Write an essay describing some of the events that have shaped our nation. Begin with an introductory paragraph, stating how past events influence the present. Your final paragraph should summarize the main ideas of your essay and give ideas about how the events discussed have shaped our nation.

Build a Model

Work with a partner to make a model. Follow these steps to make your model:

1. Choose a time you read about in Unit 1.

2. Research what the buildings and clothing looked like and what jobs people did.

3. Use materials to build a model of a building and people at work in the time period.

4. Using your research, write a description of the building and what the people are doing.

5. Present your model to the class.

EXPLORE The Big Idea

Essential Question
How do people meet their needs?

FOLDABLES™ Study Organizer

Compare and Contrast
Use a layered book foldable to take notes as you read Unit 2. Write **The United States** on the cover. Label the three tabs **Geography**, **Economy**, and **Government**. Use the foldable to organize information.

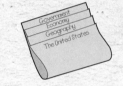

Government
Economy
Geography
The United States

LOG ON
For more about Unit 2 go to
www.macmillanmh.com

The United States: Its Land and People

PEOPLE, PLACES, and EVENTS

Madam C.J. Walker

The Walker Building

Madam C.J. Walker was the first African American female millionaire. In the early 1900s, she started her own hair care and cosmetics business with just a few dollars.

Today the Walker Building in Indianapolis, Indiana, houses the Madam Walker Theater Center.

Donna House

Smithsonian Folklife Festival

The Smithsonian Institution is the world's largest museum complex. The grounds of its newest museum, the National Museum of the American Indian, were designed by **Donna House**.

Today visit the museums and attend festivals such as the **Smithsonian Folklife Festival** in Washington, D.C.

Americans Vote

Soldiers Vote

Americans vote in national, state, and local elections. Voting is an important part of being a good citizen. Even **soldiers vote** in special stations set up just for overseas military people.

Today visit the National Museum of American History in Washington, D.C., to learn more about voting's history.

The United States Mint

Mint Workers

The **United States Mint** makes coins used in the United States. **Mint workers** inspect all the coins before the money goes into circulation.

Today you can tour the mint in Denver, Colorado, or Philadelphia, Pennsylvania, and see how money is made.

THE UNITED STATES

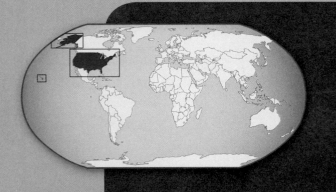

The United States has many historic and beautiful places to visit.

1 Mt. Hood is a volcano and also the tallest mountain in Oregon.

6 Cowboy boots are a symbol of the American West. They help cowboys stay secure in their saddles.

5 The Saguaro can live up to 200 years. Its side arms grow to absorb water.

WA
Columbia R.
1 Mt. Hood
OR
COLUMBIA PLATEAU
CASCADE RANGE
COAST RANGES
SIERRA NEVADA
CENTRAL VALLEY
Lake Tahoe
GREAT BASIN
NV
San Francisco Bay
CA
Lake Mead
MOJAVE DESERT
Salton Sea
Colorado River
5

HI
PACIFIC OCEAN
N W E S
0   100   200 miles
0   100 200 kilometers

PACIFIC OCEAN

Inset map (Alaska)

ARCTIC OCEAN

RUSSIA

BROOKS RANGE

AK

CANADA

ALASKA RANGE

Yukon River

Gulf of Alaska

Aleutian Islands

0   400 miles

0   400 kilometers

2 The Gateway Arch in St. Louis, Missouri, marks the city as the "Gateway to the West."

3 The Capitol Building is in Washington, D.C.

Main map

CANADA

Missouri River

MT

ND

GREAT

MESABI RANGE

MN

Lake Superior

GREAT LAKES

St. La

ME

VT

NH

ROCKY

6

SD

Mississippi River

WI

Lake Huron

Lake Ontario

ADIRONDACK MOUNTAINS

MA

RI

BLACK HILLS

WY

IA

CENTRAL PLAINS

MI

Lake Michigan

Lake Erie

NY

CT

Great Salt Lake

NE

Platte River

River

IL

IN

OH

Ohio River

PA

WV

MD

DE

NJ

Washington, D.C.

Chesapeake Bay

GREAT SALT LAKE DESERT

UT

CO

KS

Arkansas River

MO

St. Louis

2

KY

VA

PIEDMONT

ATLANTIC COASTAL PLAIN

3

MOUNTAINS

COLORADO PLATEAU

INTERIOR PLAINS

OZARK PLATEAU

TN

Tennessee River

NC

APPALACHIAN MOUNTAINS

AZ

NM

Pecos River

OK

AR

OUACHITA MOUNTAINS

Red River

MS

AL

SC

GA

Savannah River

ATLANTIC OCEAN

SONORAN DESERT

TX

Brazos River

Colorado River

LA

Mississippi River

Chattahoochee River

Alabama River

N

EDWARDS PLATEAU

Rio Grande

GULF COASTAL PLAIN

Mobile Bay

FL

4

Galveston Bay

MEXICO

Gulf of Mexico

0   200   400 miles

0   200   400 kilometers

4 The American Alligator is only found in the Southeast. They can grow up to 19 feet long!

Lesson 1

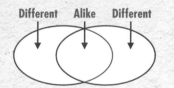
From Sea to Sea

The United States has many kinds of landforms.

Visual Preview

How have people in the United States adapted to geography?

A The United States has a wide variety of landforms.

B In the East are coastal plains, the Appalachian Mountains, and interior plains.

C The West has the Rocky Mountains, plateaus, and dry deserts.

D There are many different habitats and environments in our country.

A A VARIED LAND

If you could soar like an eagle across the United States, you'd fly over snowcapped mountains and across sunbaked deserts. You'd spot mighty rivers and lakes that stretch farther than an eagle's eye can see. You'd see forests, hills, plains, and more.

Our country is big! It's almost 3,000 miles from coast to coast. There are all sorts of landforms—the shapes that make up Earth's surface—including mountains, hills, valleys, and flatlands, or plains.

There is water, too. The Atlantic Ocean is on our east coast and the Pacific Ocean is on our west coast. Large cities have grown up along the coasts at harbors where ships can be protected. Besides the oceans, there are thousands of rivers, streams, and lakes throughout the countryside.

Our country has many resources—rich farmlands, forests of tall trees, coal and oil, and **minerals** such as iron, silver, copper, and gold. A mineral is a resource found in nature. In each part of our country, people have learned to use these resources to supply the things they need to live.

Let's fly over the country and take a look at our water, landforms, and natural resources.

QUICK CHECK

Compare and Contrast How are Denali and Death Valley different?

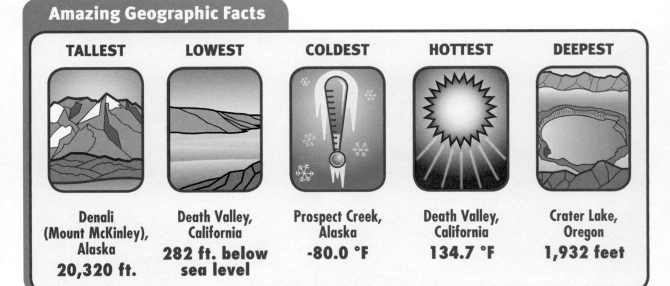

Amazing Geographic Facts

TALLEST	LOWEST	COLDEST	HOTTEST	DEEPEST
Denali (Mount McKinley), Alaska **20,320 ft.**	Death Valley, California **282 ft. below sea level**	Prospect Creek, Alaska **-80.0 °F**	Death Valley, California **134.7 °F**	Crater Lake, Oregon **1,932 feet**

B   IN THE EAST

Let's start the flight at the Atlantic coast. What will you see in the East? Use the map as you read to follow along.

Along the Coast

In most places, the land along the coast is low and flat. This is the coastal plain. As you fly, you see many beaches of golden sand, but there are places where the waves crash against rocky shores.

When settlers first came here from Europe, they settled on this coastal plain. The plains were covered with forests then, but little by little the settlers cut down the forests to make farms and to build towns. Today most of the forests are gone.

The Appalachian Mountains

As you move inland away from the coastal plain, you come to the Appalachian Mountains. These are very old mountains. Once they had high, sharp peaks. Over the years, they've been worn down by **erosion**. Erosion is the wearing away of Earth's surface. Millions of years of wind, water, and ice have made the mountains rounded and lower.

Farming is not easy here, but these mountains are rich in coal. Many people came to the mountains of Pennsylvania and West Virginia to make a living mining coal.

The Blue Ridge Mountains are part of the Appalachian Mountains.

Across the Plains

West of the Appalachians, the land is flat again. This is the interior plain. The rich soil here makes it one of the best places in the United States for farming. You look down on colorful fields, like a patchwork quilt of wheat, corn, soybeans, and other crops.

Great Lakes and Long Rivers

From up above, the Great Lakes look like giant puddles. This area was once covered by thick sheets of ice. When the ice melted, it formed the Great Lakes.

The lakes are important routes for transportation and shipping. That's why cities such as Chicago, Cleveland, and Detroit were built along their shores.

Next you'll cross over the Mississippi River, our country's longest river. Many **tributaries**, or smaller rivers, flow into the Mississippi. People have used the Mississippi River for transportation for thousands of years.

QUICK CHECK

Cause and Effect How were the Great Lakes formed?

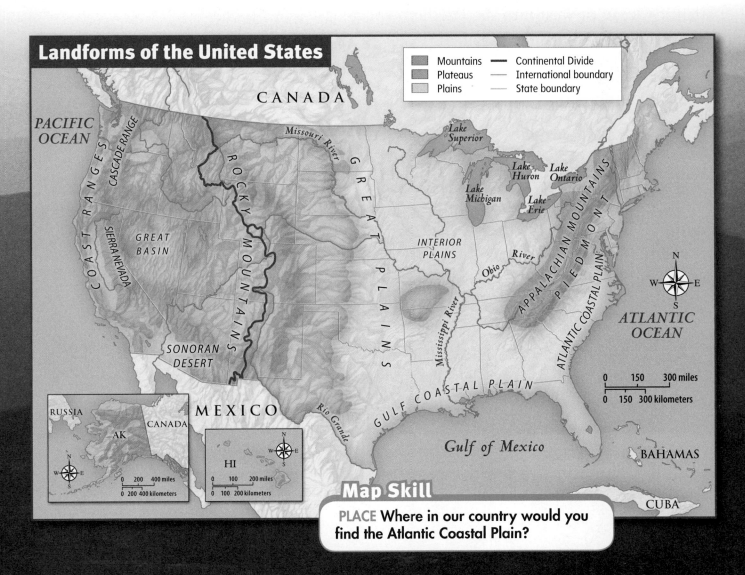

Landforms of the United States

	Mountains	—— Continental Divide
	Plateaus	International boundary
	Plains	State boundary

CANADA

PACIFIC OCEAN

CASCADE RANGE

COAST RANGES

SIERRA NEVADA

GREAT BASIN

ROCKY MOUNTAINS

SONORAN DESERT

Missouri River

GREAT PLAINS

INTERIOR PLAINS

Lake Superior

Lake Huron

Lake Michigan

Lake Ontario

Lake Erie

Ohio River

APPALACHIAN MOUNTAINS

PIEDMONT

ATLANTIC COASTAL PLAIN

ATLANTIC OCEAN

Mississippi River

GULF COASTAL PLAIN

MEXICO

Rio Grande

Gulf of Mexico

BAHAMAS

CUBA

RUSSIA

CANADA

AK

HI

0   200   400 miles
0 200 400 kilometers

0 100 200 miles
0 100 200 kilometers

0   150   300 miles
0 150 300 kilometers

Map Skill

PLACE **Where in our country would you find the Atlantic Coastal Plain?**

As you travel west of the Mississippi River, the land rises. Now you are on the Great Plains. It is drier, and there are few trees. These vast plains are good places to raise cattle or grow wheat and corn.

The plains seem endless, but then you see the Rocky Mountains. The Rockies stretch from Alaska to New Mexico. They are higher, sharper, and they formed thousands of years after the Appalachians. From their topmost ridge, rivers and streams flow either east into the Atlantic Ocean or west into the Pacific Ocean. This dividing ridge is called the Continental Divide.

Highlands and Lowlands

Beyond the Rockies, there are several large plateaus. A **plateau** is a high, flat area that rises steeply from the land around it. The huge Great Basin covers parts of Nevada and several other states. A **basin** is a low landform—the opposite of a plateau. It is shaped like a bowl and surrounded by higher land. The Great Basin gets very little rain, so it's a desert. People who live there have learned to use water wisely.

Saguaro cactuses grow in the deserts of the Southwest.

▲ Many wildflowers grow in the Rocky Mountains.

Next, you come to even more mountain ranges—the Cascades in the north, and the Sierra Nevada in California. When you reach the Pacific Ocean your journey across the United States is almost over.

Alaska and Hawaii

To find Alaska, you fly northward along the coast through Canada until you see the snow-covered Alaska Range. Here, you find the country's tallest mountain, Denali (Mount McKinley). As you near the Arctic Ocean, the land becomes low and flat again.

To reach Hawaii, you must fly out over the Pacific Ocean. Hawaii is a chain of islands that were formed by volcanoes on the ocean floor. Once, Hawaii was an independent nation. Its last ruler was Queen Liliuokalani. Many people visit Hawaii to enjoy its warm weather and beautiful beaches.

QUICK CHECK

Compare and Contrast What is the difference between a basin and a plateau?

Hawaii has beautiful beaches.

PEOPLE

Queen Liliuokalani was the last ruler of the Hawaiian Islands. She was forced to give up her throne before Hawaii became part of the United States in 1898.

Queen Liliuokalani

Palm trees grow where it is warm.

75

D MANY ENVIRONMENTS

Because our country is so large, land and weather can vary from place to place. There are also many different kinds of ecosystems. An ecosystem is all of the things, living and nonliving, in a certain area. It is like a nature neighborhood. The air, the water, and the soil in each place are all part of the ecosystem.

Each member of the ecosystem depends on the other members. Each has adapted in order to survive in its environment. For instance, deer and raccoons live in the rainy woodlands of the Appalachian Mountains. Lizards and jackrabbits live among cacti in the Great Basin.

People are also part of an ecosystem. As people move and settle in new places in our country, they learn to use the plant, animal, and mineral resources they find. They learn to use different farming methods, or to grow different crops. Like the animals and plants, they learn to adapt to meet their needs in their environment.

QUICK CHECK

Cause and Effect Why are animals different in each ecosystem?

This moose lives in the woodlands of the East.

Check Understanding

1. **VOCABULARY** Draw a picture to illustrate each word below. Label each picture.
   tributary   **plateau**   **basin**

2. **READING SKILL Compare and Contrast** Use your chart from page 70 to write about the eastern and western parts of our country.

3. **Write About It** Write about ways people use the different landforms of the United States to meet their needs.

Map and Globe Skills

Use Elevation Maps

VOCABULARY

elevation

sea level

How would you know which state has the highest mountains? For this kind of information, you need an **elevation** map. Elevation is the height of land above **sea level**, or the level of the surface at the sea. Elevation at sea level is zero feet.

Learn It

- Elevation maps use colors to show the height, or elevation, of land. Not all maps show the same elevation levels.

- The map key tells what each color on the map stands for, in both feet and meters.

Try It

- Which state has a higher elevation, Illinois or New Mexico?

- What states have elevations above 5,000 feet?

Apply It

- Compare the elevations of the states along the Atlantic Coast with the states along the Pacific Coast.

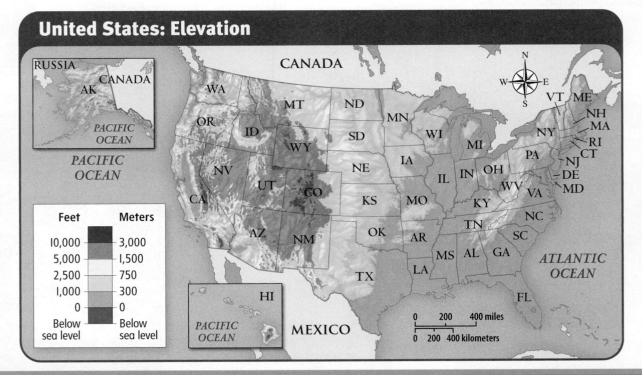

United States: Elevation

Feet	Meters
10,000	3,000
5,000	1,500
2,500	750
1,000	300
0	0
Below sea level	Below sea level

Our Country's Regions

Lesson 2

VOCABULARY

region p. 79

economy p. 82

agriculture p. 82

interdependent p. 82

READING SKILL

Compare and Contrast
Copy the chart. Fill it in with facts about our country's regions.

Different   Alike   Different

STANDARDS FOCUS

SOCIAL STUDIES People, Places, and Environments

GEOGRAPHY Places and Regions

The building styles in the Southwest show the region's Spanish history.

Visual Preview

How are regions affected by natural resources?

A Regions can be described by geography or culture.

B Regions of the United States share natural and economic resources.

C States in a region work together to protect their resources.

Ⓐ WHAT IS A REGION?

Our country is so varied that it's hard to describe. It has highlands and lowlands, cold winters and warm winters. It all depends on what part of the country you are talking about.

The United States is a large country, so it makes sense that one place in our country can be very different from another. To help us understand our country more easily, we divide it into **regions**, or groups of states with common features.

Kinds of Regions

One kind of region is a geographic region. A geographic region shares similar landforms and climates. There are mountain regions, plains regions, and desert regions.

Other kinds of regions are cultural regions. This means they are based on human features, such as history or language. For instance, the states of the Southwest share a history. They were once part of Mexico.

If you visit the Southeast, you might eat southern fried chicken or hear gospel music on the radio. You might notice that people there speak a little differently than people in the North or in the West. All these things—food, music, language, even holidays and customs—are part of culture, the way of life that a people share. A common culture can make an area a region, too.

QUICK CHECK

Compare and Contrast How are geographic regions and cultural regions different?

The people of the Southwest share many customs. ▶

ONE COUNTRY, FIVE REGIONS

Look at the five regions of the United States on the map. These regions are based on geographic features such as landforms and climate. They're based on human features such as history and culture. Each region's geography, economy, and people are unique.

Shared Resources

Natural resources, such as forests or rivers, don't usually stop at state borders. States in a region share many of the same resources. Since the resources are important, states work together to protect them. Suppose a river runs through several states. If one state passes laws to stop pollution, but the other states don't pass similar laws, it won't help the river.

The Mississippi River is home to many kinds of wildlife, including this Great Blue Heron.

The Mississippi River is an important resource for many states. Ron Kind is a government leader in Wisconsin. He is concerned about taking care of the river.

❝We could work together . . . to draw attention to the resources that are needed along the Mississippi River.❞

Clean air is important, too. In the Northeast, for example, states are working together to pass laws to fight air pollution that affects all of them.

QUICK CHECK

Summarize Besides landforms, what are some other things that states in a region may share?

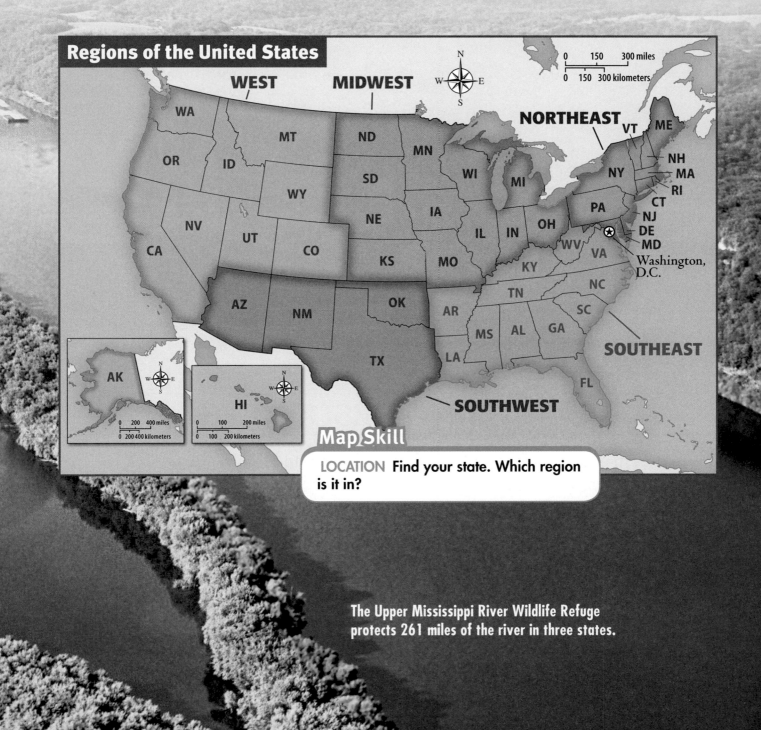

Regions of the United States

WEST

MIDWEST

NORTHEAST

SOUTHEAST

SOUTHWEST

WA
MT
OR
ID
ND
MN
SD
WY
NE
IA
NV
UT
CO
CA
AZ
NM
KS
MO
OK
TX
AR
LA
WI
MI
IL
IN
OH
WV
KY
TN
MS
AL
GA
VA
NC
SC
FL
PA
NY
VT
ME
NH
MA
RI
CT
NJ
DE
MD
Washington, D.C.

AK

HI

0 150 300 miles
0 150 300 kilometers

0 200 400 miles
0 200 400 kilometers

0 100 200 miles
0 100 200 kilometers

Map Skill

LOCATION **Find your state. Which region is it in?**

The Upper Mississippi River Wildlife Refuge protects 261 miles of the river in three states.

▲ Mining coal is important to the economy of the Southeast, but other parts of the country also depend on the Southeast's coal.

ⓒ USING RESOURCES

Since states in a region often share resources, they usually share an **economy**. This makes sense when you think that the economy is the way a region uses its resources to provide the things that people need. For example, **agriculture**, or farming, is very important in almost every state of the Midwest.

Another example is the coal-mining in the states of the Appalachian Mountains.

Mining is an important part of how people there make a living. So the people in this region share the same concerns. Since the states in this region share an economy, the people in those states are linked together.

Resources Link Regions

Today, states and regions are **interdependent**, or dependent on each other. We might live in Illinois but buy

▲ In many places in the Appalachian Mountains, there is coal just underneath the surface.

oranges from Florida and grapes from California. The coal mined in Kentucky provides energy for people in other regions. Mining links the people of the Southeast to each other and to the rest of the country.

QUICK CHECK

Summarize How does sharing resources in a region make states interdependent?

Check Understanding

1. **VOCABULARY** Create a poster about your region. Be sure to illustrate each of the vocabulary words in your poster.

   region   economy   agriculture

2. **READING SKILL Compare and Contrast** Use your diagram from page 78 to write about how geographic regions and cultural regions are alike and different.

3. **Write About It** Write a paragraph about how people use a region's resources.

Our Country's Climate

VOCABULARY

precipitation p 86

rain shadow p. 87

lake effect p. 88

tornado p. 90

hurricane p. 90

READING SKILL

Compare and Contrast
Copy the diagram. Use it to compare and contrast the climate of places in the lesson.

Different   Alike   Different

STANDARDS FOCUS

SOCIAL STUDIES People, Places, and Environments

GEOGRAPHY Physical Systems

The climate near Mount Hood in Oregon is good for growing pears and apples.

Visual Preview

How does climate affect people in the United States?

A Distance from the equator and elevation affect climate.

B Mountains affect where rain falls.

C The climate in an area is based on temperature and precipitation.

D Some places get extreme weather.

WEATHER AND CLIMATE

It's 10 degrees Fahrenheit outside on a typical winter day in Wisconsin. Meanwhile, it's 75 degrees in Florida! It's hard to believe both places are in the same country.

How's the weather today? Is it hot or cold? Is it raining? Weather describes the air and the temperature at a certain time and place. Climate is a little different. Climate is the pattern of weather over time—the kind of weather a place *usually* has.

Temperature

The temperature is cold at the North and South Poles and hot at the equator. As you move away from the poles and closer to the equator, temperatures get warmer. The southern part of our country is closer to the equator, so temperatures there are usually warmer than in the North.

Elevation also affects temperature. The higher up a mountain you go, the colder it gets. Places at high elevations are usually colder than places at low elevations.

On a spring day in Portland you might be comfortable outdoors wearing just a T-shirt. On the same day, only a few miles away at the top of Mt. Hood (11,234 feet high), you'd need a warm coat and mittens!

QUICK CHECK

Compare and Contrast How do temperatures at the North Pole and the equator differ?

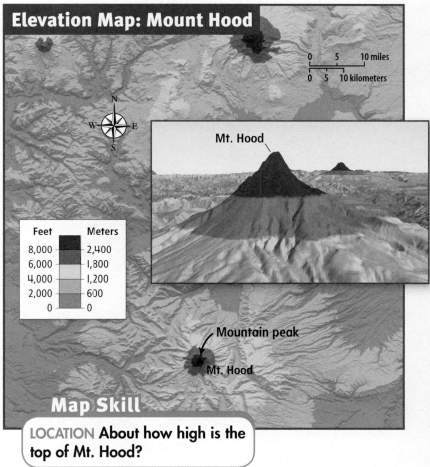

Elevation Map: Mount Hood

| 0 | 5 | 10 miles |
| 0 | 5 | 10 kilometers |

Mt. Hood

Feet	Meters
8,000	2,400
6,000	1,300
4,000	1,200
2,000	600
0	0

Mountain peak

Mt. Hood

Map Skill

LOCATION About how high is the top of Mt. Hood?

WATER AND CLIMATE

Rain, rain, go away! Did you learn this rhyme when you were little? If you live in an area with very little **precipitation**, you might want the rain to fall. Precipitation is the moisture that falls to the ground as rain, sleet, snow, or hail.

Mountains and Rainfall

2 Clouds form.

3 When air reaches the mountains, it rises and cools.

1 The winds blowing in from the ocean usually carry a lot of moisture.

4 As the air cools, the moisture in the clouds turns into rain or snow. The side of the mountain that faces the ocean gets a lot of rain or snow.

Mountains and Rainfall

How do mountains affect rainfall? We say the side of the mountain that faces away from the ocean is in the **rain shadow**. The western slopes of Oregon's Cascade Mountains can get 200 inches of precipitation a year. Only a few dozen miles to the east, the other side of the mountains gets less than 8 inches of precipitation a year.

QUICK CHECK

Cause and Effect Why does the eastern side of the mountains in Oregon get very little rain or snow?

5 The side of the mountain away from the ocean might get very little rain or snow. By the time the winds cross over the mountain, almost all the moisture has fallen.

ⓒ LAKES AND SNOW

If you like snow, you might want to move to Houghton, Michigan, on Lake Superior. It gets an average of 177 inches of snow per year! Another snowy city is Rochester, New York, on Lake Ontario.

The reason these two cities get so much snow is something called **lake effect**. Large bodies of water such as big lakes or the ocean affect the climate of the land near them. How does this happen?

Lake Effect

WINTER ❶ In winter, winds blow from west to east across the Great Lakes. ❷ They pick up moisture from the lakes below. ❸ During the winter, the air over the land is usually colder than the air over the lakes. When the clouds blow over the cooler land, the moisture in the clouds is cooled, and snow falls.

SUMMER In summer, the land is warmer than the lake water. Winds blowing off the lakes bring cool air and help keep the temperatures on land from getting too high.

The weather is very different throughout the United States. However, weather tends to follow a pattern in an area. For example, in Seattle, Washington, rain usually falls between November and March, and daytime temperatures throughout the year are mild. Seattle has a wet, mild climate. Data on average temperature and average precipitation help you figure out the climate of an area.

QUICK CHECK

Cause and Effect Why do places near the Great Lakes often get a lot of snow?

DataGraphic

United States: Average January Temperatures

The map shows the average temperatures across the United States in January. The graph shows the average rainfall in specific cities. Use the map and graph to answer the questions below.

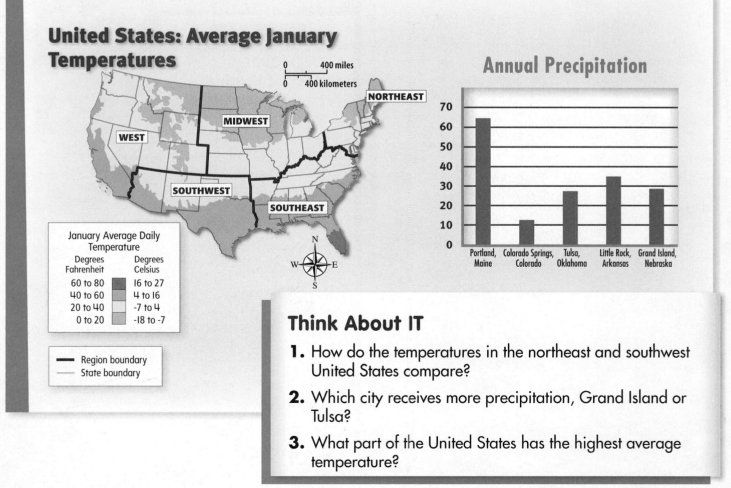

Think About IT

1. How do the temperatures in the northeast and southwest United States compare?
2. Which city receives more precipitation, Grand Island or Tulsa?
3. What part of the United States has the highest average temperature?

D EXTREME WEATHER

Some places in the United States can have extreme weather. Have you ever seen a movie called *The Wizard of Oz?* In that movie, a **tornado** picks up a girl named Dorothy and carries her off to a land called Oz. The movie is only a story, but tornadoes are real. A tornado is a strong wind that forms a funnel shape and moves over the ground very quickly, destroying everything in its path. Sometimes, tornadoes are powerful enough to pick up and move cars!

Tornadoes can happen anywhere in the United States, but they occur more often where cold air from Canada meets warm air coming up from the Gulf of Mexico.

This area is called Tornado Alley, and it runs from central Texas through Oklahoma, Kansas, Nebraska, and Iowa.

Hurricanes are another kind of extreme weather. A hurricane is a storm with very strong winds and heavy rain. Hurricanes form over the warm water in the Atlantic Ocean to the south of the United States. As hurricanes move north, some of them may hit land in the Southeast.

Hurricane winds push water in front of them. The wind and water can be very dangerous and can cause terrible damage.

EVENT

In August 2005, **Hurricane Katrina** slammed into the Gulf Coast. It was one of the strongest hurricanes ever recorded to hit the United States. As a result of the storm, most of New Orleans flooded and many people died.

Rebuilding after Hurricane Katrina

Climate and Storms

There were a record number of hurricanes in the United States in 2005. One of them, Hurricane Katrina, caused a lot of damage in New Orleans and other communities on the Gulf of Mexico.

Most scientists think that Earth's climate is growing warmer, heating the ocean waters and causing more severe storms. Scientists are studying weather patterns and learning new ways to predict hurricanes and other storms.

◀ A tornado rips through South Dakota.

QUICK CHECK

Compare and Contrast **What is the difference between a hurricane and a tornado?**

Check Understanding

1. **VOCABULARY** Draw a picture to illustrate each word. Label the picture.

   tornado   rain shadow   lake effect

2. **READING SKILL Compare and Contrast** Use the chart from page 84 to compare the temperature at the top of a mountain with the temperature at the mountain's base.

3. **Write About It** Write about the climate where you live. Then give two examples of ways people in your town have adapted to the climate.

Lesson 4

RUNNING A BUSINESS

VOCABULARY
profit p. 94

investor p. 95

supply p. 95

demand p. 95

opportunity cost p. 97

READING SKILL
Compare and Contrast
Copy the chart. Fill it in with facts about the advertising and sales departments.

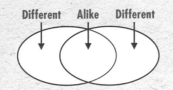

Different   Alike   Different

STANDARDS FOCUS

| SOCIAL STUDIES | Production, Distribution, and Consumption |
| GEOGRAPHY | Human Systems |

Mrs. High's fourth grade class decided to start its own business.

Visual Preview

What do people think about when they start a business?

A In the free-enterprise system, anyone can start their own businesses.

B Producers must make many choices.

C People work together to run a business.

Ⓐ   A BIG DECISION

Did you ever dream of starting your own business? A group of elementary students in Missouri did. They ran a business called Popcorn Mania. Here's how they got their start.

Early in January, 4th grade teacher Mrs. High called a class meeting. She told her students that they had a big decision to make. They had to decide if they wanted to start a business. They talked about the work involved in making and selling a product. The students voted to do it. They would sell popcorn. They would call their new company "Popcorn Mania."

Starting a Business

How is it that students in an elementary school can start a business? Well, every country in the world has a system it uses for money. Some countries have a planned economy in which one organization makes all economic decisions. Other countries, such as the United States, use the free-enterprise system. An enterprise is something that a person plans or tries to do. Our economy is called free enterprise because anyone is allowed to start a business, even the class at Meadow Lane Elementary.

A free enterprise economy also lets us decide what to buy based on what we want or need and how much we want to pay. No one tells us how to spend our money. In a free enterprise system everyone makes his or her own economic decisions.

QUICK CHECK

Compare and Contrast What is the difference between a planned economy and a free enterprise system?

93

THE FACTS ABOUT BUSINESS

When the class decided to start a business, they became entrepreneurs. Entrepreneurs are people who set up and run their own businesses. Before they started, they thought about what people might need or want. They thought about a service, or way of doing something.

Entrepreneurs take risks by creating products or offering services they think people will buy. If a business does well, an entrepreneur makes a **profit**. That's the money left over after a business pays for supplies, tools, and workers' salaries. In other words—it's all the extra money.

Getting Organized

Once the class agreed to start a business, they had to figure out how to get things done. They decided to divide into groups, each responsible for something different. This is called specialization. The groups were sales, advertising, production (making the product), and finance (working with money). They were interdependent. They needed one another.

The finance department bought the popcorn from a local business for $32 a barrel. They bought 11 barrels. How much did all of that cost? More money than they had! To buy the popcorn, they needed to raise money.

The production department made the product. ▼

▲ The sales and advertising departments worked together to bring in customers.

Money Matters

Starting a business costs money. Many new businesses borrow money from an **investor**, which is a person or company that puts money into a business and expects to get some of the profit in return. If the business doesn't do well, the investor may lose all the money he or she invested.

The main investor in Popcorn Mania was a local bank. The bank agreed to loan the class the money to buy the popcorn. The bank, like most investors, expected the money to be paid back.

Then, students had to decide on a price for their product. They used what they knew about **supply** and **demand** to make this decision. They knew that they had enough supply (the popcorn), but did they have enough demand? Would their fellow schoolmates want or even be able to buy the popcorn? The students wanted to set a price that other students could afford. The price needed to cover the cost of their supplies. They decided on 50 cents a bag.

QUICK CHECK

Main Idea and Details How did the class organize the business?

The production department bought the popcorn. Then, they made their product. They made 2,100 bags of popcorn. That's a lot of popcorn! It took them about 5 days.

The advertising department had to find ways to let consumers (people who buy a product) know about their product. They made posters and even a short video for classrooms.

The sales department set up a table near the school cafeteria. Some students greeted the customers and took their orders. Others handed the orders over to the customers or collected money. The sale lasted for 5 days. The students sold almost $1,000 worth of popcorn. After they paid all their expenses, the class earned more than $600 in profit.

The Key to Success

Success in business requires teamwork, a desire to do the best work possible, and goals. That's how the students at Meadow Lane Elementary School succeeded with Popcorn Mania. Any business—from a lemonade stand to a large corporation—can succeed keeping these things in mind. See what John D. Rockefeller, the world's first billionaire, had to say about success.

Primary Sources

"The secret of success is to do the common things uncommonly well."

—John D. Rockefeller

Write About It Write a sentence describing your secret to success.

The finance department of Popcorn Mania helped decide how the class would spend its profits.

One More Decision

After the class repaid their loan to the bank, they used some of the profit for a field trip. Then, the students had to decide what to do with the rest of the money.

They discussed the **opportunity cost** of each choice they might make. When you decide to buy one thing, you are giving up the chance to buy other things. This is the opportunity cost. The class could go on another field trip or buy kits for making kites. They decided to buy the kites. The opportunity cost was the trip.

Working Together

The students learned a lot about running a business. The most important lesson of all was this: for a business to be successful people must work together.

QUICK CHECK

Summarize What choices did the students have about using the profit from their business?

Check Understanding

1. **VOCABULARY** Summarize this lesson using these vocabulary words.
   supply   **demand**

2. **READING SKILL Compare and Contrast** Use your chart from page 93 to write a sentence about the sales department.

3. **Write About It** Write a paragraph about how your community meets its needs in the free enterprise system.

VOCABULARY

producer p. 100

capital resource p. 101

human resource p. 101

natural resource p. 101

interest p. 102

credit p. 102

READING SKILL

Compare and Contrast
Copy the chart. Fill it in
with needs and wants.

Different   Alike   Different

STANDARDS FOCUS

SOCIAL STUDIES Production, Distribution, and Consumption

GEOGRAPHY Human Systems

This boy is shopping for
something he wants but
doesn't need.

Our Economy

Visual Preview

How do resources affect the economic choices people make?

A Needs, wants, and scarcity are important parts of our economy.

B Businesses use natural resources, human resources, and capital resources.

C Banks loan money. People save money in a bank to earn interest.

D Businesses and consumers all play a role in our economy.

Ⓐ NEEDS AND WANTS

What do you really need to live? Food? A DVD player? A home?
We call things like food, clothing, and shelter needs.
You can't live without them. Once you have met the most
basic needs, everything else is a want.

Wants are things you can live without. You don't need a DVD player or a pair of $100 sneakers to live, do you? You can make your own music and buy an inexpensive pair of sneakers. Wants might make your life easier or more interesting, but you can live without them.

Scarcity

Now that you know the difference between what you need and what you want, let's talk about scarcity—when there isn't enough of what you need or want. Scarcity comes from the word scarce, which describes something that is hard to find or is in short supply. You could have a scarcity of money or a scarcity of a nonrenewable resource. For example, sometimes the world has a scarcity of oil.

When there is a scarcity of something, the price of the item usually goes up. Why? The price goes up because people will pay more for something that they want if it's hard to find.

In 2000, for example, the average price of a barrel of oil was $28. Due in part to scarcity, the average price went up to $62 a barrel in 2002. The price more than doubled in just a few years.

QUICK CHECK

Compare and Contrast What is the difference between needs and wants?

During a gas shortage in Houston, Texas, gas prices more than doubled at many stations. ▶

Farmer

Blacksmith

In the 1700s, people traded goods or services for things they needed.

Ⓑ THE BASICS OF OUR ECONOMY

In the early days of our country, money was scarce. People grew or made just about everything they needed. Sometimes, people would grow or make a little extra of something. Then they might barter, or trade, for something they didn't have or could not grow or make.

Someone who was good at making one thing, might make them for everyone in the village in return for payment. A shoemaker might make shoes for everyone that he knew. Making shoes was that person's specialization.

People still bartered, though. The shoemaker might be paid with a couple of chickens, some soap, or a bag of grain. As businesses grew, people hired other workers to help them manufacture, or make large numbers of goods to sell.

People who make goods are called **producers**. They sell the products to consumers, the people who use them. But producers need things as well. At some point, everyone is a consumer. When you buy a hamburger, a computer game, or a movie ticket, you are a consumer, too.

Business Resource	Description
Capital Resources 	**Capital resources** are all the things businesses use to make, produce, or transport a good or service. They include computers, printers, machines, or even factories.
Natural Resources 	**Natural resources** are needed by many businesses. Farmers need soil to grow crops, computer manufacturers use metal to build their machines, and stores are heated with oil or natural gas.
Human Resources 	**Human resources** are the people who work for a business. Mail carriers are part of the human resources of the postal service. Teachers are part of the human resources of schools.

Chart Skill

How are capital resources different from human resources?

Business Resources

What would you need to run a business? Of course it depends on the kind of business you'd be running. You've learned that businesses need money to pay for all sorts of things to keep them going.

Businesses need other things to be successful. A business's spending can be broken down into three main categories—capital resources, natural resources, and human resources. The chart above shows the resources needed for a business. What kind of resource is a truck for a delivery business? What resource is the driver?

QUICK CHECK

Summarize What are the three kinds of resources described in this section?

D CARING FOR THE ECONOMY

Circular Flow

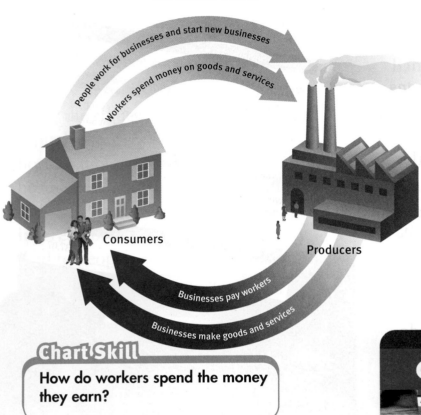

People work for businesses and start new businesses

Workers spend money on goods and services

Consumers

Producers

Businesses pay workers

Businesses make goods and services

Chart Skill

How do workers spend the money they earn?

goods and services and start new businesses. The Circular Flow chart on this page shows how money moves through our economy.

QUICK CHECK

Draw Conclusions How is the economy helped when businesses hire new workers?

Just as consumers look after their money, the United States government tracks money, too. The Federal Reserve System controls banks across the country. The United States Department of the Treasury collects taxes from workers. This is how local governments get money to build highways, schools, parks, and more.

It All Works Together

Everyone works together to make the economy run smoothly. Producers make goods and services, businesses hire workers and pay them for the jobs they do, workers use their pay to buy

Check Understanding

1. **VOCABULARY** Draw a chart that illustrates how individuals and businesses are affected by these vocabulary words. **interest** **credit**

2. **READING SKILL Compare and Contrast** Use your chart from page 99 to write about your needs and wants.

Different Alike Different

3. **Write About It** Write a paragraph about the businesses in your community. What do they do?
EXPLORE The Big Idea

Chart and Graph Skills

Read Line Graphs

VOCABULARY
graph
line graph

The number of computers sold in our country has changed over time. One way to learn how it has changed is to look at a **graph**. Graphs are diagrams that show information in a clear way. **Line graphs** show change over time.

Learn It

● The line graph at the top shows how the number of personal computers sold in the United States changed between 1997 and 2005.

● Labels on the side of each graph tell you the number of people. Labels on the bottom show the year. The top graph shows every other year.

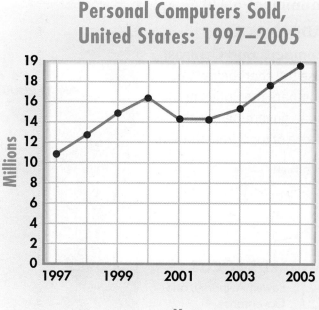

Personal Computers Sold, United States: 1997–2005

Try It

● Look at the top line graph. How many personal computers were sold in 1997?

● In what year did the sale of personal computers go down?

Apply It

● Look at the bottom line graph. Write two sentences based on the information shown on the graph.

● How can line graphs help you to compare and contrast information?

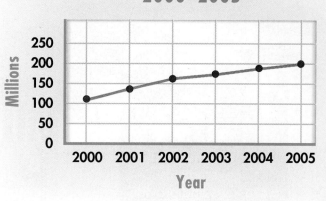

Internet Users, United States: 2000–2005

STATE AND LOCAL GOVERNMENTS

VOCABULARY

constitution p. 108

legislative branch p.108

executive branch p.108

judicial branch p. 108

veto p. 109

municipal p. 110

READING SKILL

Compare and Contrast
Use the chart below to compare the duties of state government with those of local government.

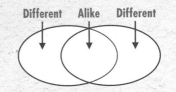

Different   Alike   Different

STANDARDS FOCUS

SOCIAL STUDIES Power, Authority, and Governance

GEOGRAPHY Human Systems

Local governments provide firefighters that protect our towns and cities.

Visual Preview

Why do state and local governments work together?

A State and local governments make laws and provide services.

B The three branches in state governments each have different powers.

C Local governments provide services, make laws, and collect taxes.

A SHARING POWER

On the way to school, you notice that the traffic light isn't working at a busy intersection. Who should you call to get the traffic light fixed? Would you call the President to fix a traffic light?

Maybe you've heard someone say, "The government should do something about that!" What exactly is the government, anyway?

The President is just one part of the government. A government is the people and laws that run a town, county, state, or country. In the United States, government responsibilities are shared. One person, or even one group, does not run everything. States, counties, cities, and towns all have their own governments. These smaller governments create laws and provide services for smaller areas. They share power and responsibility.

Some government duties belong to the states. Others belong to towns and cities. Look at the chart to see the duties each level of government takes care of.

QUICK CHECK

Compare and Contrast How are the different levels of government the same? How are they different?

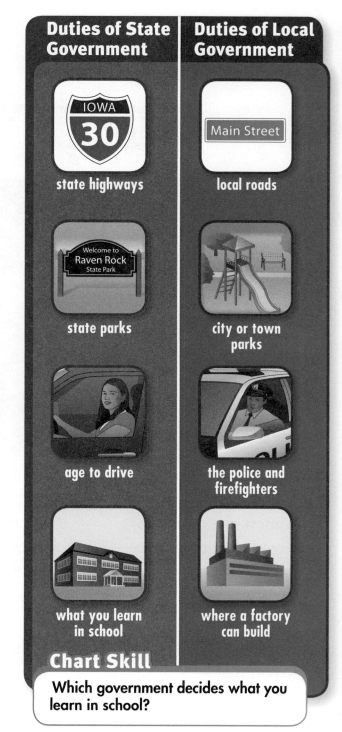

Duties of State Government	Duties of Local Government
state highways	local roads
state parks	city or town parks
age to drive	the police and firefighters
what you learn in school	where a factory can build

Chart Skill

Which government decides what you learn in school?

HOW STATE GOVERNMENTS WORK

Each state has its own **constitution**, or plan of government, and laws. Running a state is a big job. The constitution of a state divides state governments into three branches, or parts. The branches work together to run the state. No branch has total control. This system of sharing power is called checks and balances.

Study the charts to see what the branches do and to see how a bill becomes a law.

Cause and Effect What can the state court do if it thinks a law is wrong?

Three Jobs, Three Branches

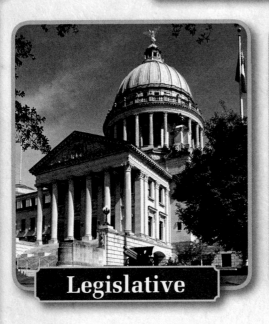

Legislative

Executive

Judicial

The **legislative branch** makes the laws. Most legislatures have two parts—an assembly and a senate. Voters in most states elect both state senators and assembly members.

The governor is head of the **executive branch**. He or she is the highest elected state official. The governor plans the state budget and decides whether to sign a bill into law.

The **judicial branch** decides whether someone has broken the law. It also interprets laws. If the state's court believes a new law goes against the state's constitution, the court can reject the law.

How a Bill Becomes Law

1. Citizens develop an idea for a bill.

2. Members of the State Assembly or the Senate propose the bill.

3. The Assembly and the Senate vote to approve the bill.

yes ☐ no ☑

4. The governor signs the bill. If he or she chooses not to sign the bill, it is called a **veto**.

5. If the bill is vetoed, another vote can be taken. If more than 2/3 of the assembly and the senate vote to approve it, the bill becomes a law.

Chart Skill

What is the first step in making a bill into a law?

C HOW LOCAL GOVERNMENTS WORK

Our country is made up of 50 states, but each state has smaller parts, usually called counties. A small state such as Connecticut has only 8 counties, while larger states have more. Arkansas, for example, has 75 counties. Each county has a government to provide services. Some county governments provide law enforcement for areas that don't have their own police department.

Cities and towns also have governments. These are called local or **municipal** governments. Some are led by mayors. Others are led by city managers, who are chosen members of the city council.

Local governments provide services and make laws. They decide how land will be used and they collect taxes. City governments provide park workers to keep the parks clean.

◄ Local government runs buses and subways.

Local government takes care of local streets, signs, and lights. ▼

◄ Park workers work for local government.

Taxes

Where do governments get money for the services they provide? Most of it comes from taxes. State governments may charge taxes on people's income. Local governments tax property and sometimes income. Homeowners pay taxes on homes and land. Some states and counties have a sales tax on goods that people buy. Businesses also pay taxes.

Tax money is used for many things. It buys equipment such as fire trucks, police cars, and stoplights. Taxes also pay the salaries of people who do jobs that maintain our cities, such as city park workers and sanitation workers.

QUICK CHECK

Summarize What are some kinds of taxes that people pay?

PLACES

This **courthouse in King William County**, Virginia, is the oldest courthouse in the country that is still in use. It was built in 1725.

King William County Courthouse

Check Understanding

1. **VOCABULARY** Write a sentence with each of the following vocabulary words.
   legislative branch   **executive branch**

2. **READING SKILL Compare and Contrast** Use your chart from page 106 to write about your local government.

3. **Write About It** Write a paragraph about how governments help people adapt to where they live.

117

Map and Globe Skills

Understand Latitude and Longitude

VOCABULARY

grid

latitude

longitude

degree

parallel

meridian

Every place on Earth has an "address" based on its location. To describe the address of a place, geographers use a map **grid**. Grids are lines that cross each other. The grid system is based on a set of lines called **latitude** and **longitude**. Lines of latitude measure how far north or south a place is from the equator. Lines of longitude measure distance east or west. Lines of latitude and longitude measure distance in **degrees**. The equator is zero degrees. The symbol for degrees is °.

Lines of Latitude

Learn It

- Lines of latitude are also called parallels. Lines of latitude north of the equator are labeled N. Lines of latitude south of the equator are labeled S.

- Lines of longitude are also called meridians. The Prime Meridian is the starting place for measuring distance from east to west. Lines of longitude east of the Prime Meridian are labeled E. Lines of longitude west of the Prime Meridian are labeled W.

- Look at Map A. Lines of longitude and latitude cross to form a global grid. It can be used to locate any place on Earth.

- To describe a location on a map, give the latitude first and the longitude second.

Lines of Longitude

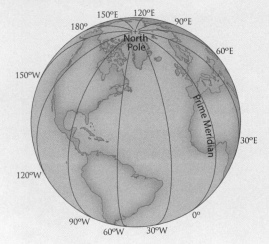

MAP A

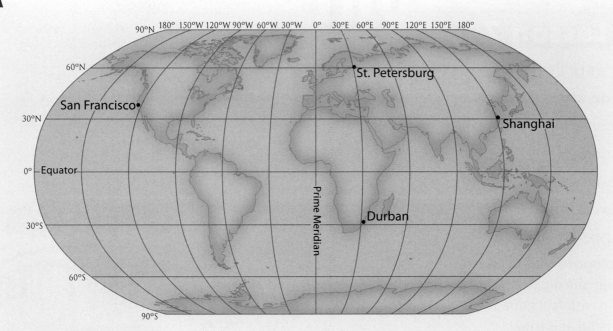

Try It

- Locate Durban, South Africa, on Map A. Durban is east of the Prime Meridian. Durban is located at about 30°S, 30°E.

Apply It

- Use Map A to locate the cities closest to these latitude and longitude addresses. Name each city.

  30°N, 120°W   60°N, 30°E

- Look at Map B. Give the latitude and longitude closest to Decatur.

MAP B

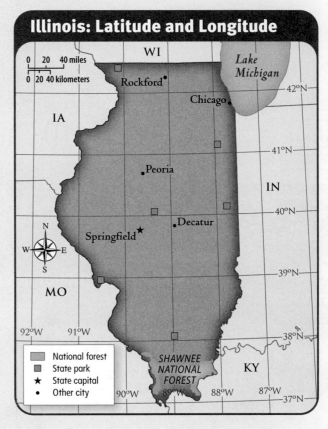

Illinois: Latitude and Longitude

	National forest
	State park
★	State capital
•	Other city

Our Nation's Government

VOCABULARY

federal p. 115

democracy p. 115

citizen p. 115

reservation p. 119

sovereign p. 119

READING SKILL

Compare and Contrast
Copy the diagram. Fill it in with facts about federal and tribal government.

Different   Alike   Different

STANDARDS FOCUS

SOCIAL STUDIES — Power, Authority, and Governance.

GEOGRAPHY — Human Systems

The United States Capitol.

We the People

Visual Preview

How has the national government adapted to meet people's needs?

A The United States is a democracy. Citizens elect leaders to represent them.

B The United States government has three branches.

C Many Native Americans have their own tribal governments.

A   OUR NATIONAL GOVERNMENT

The United States Constitution begins with "We the People." That shows that "the people" control the government. That includes you! What are some ways that our government represents the people?

The government of the United States is called the national, or **federal**, government. It provides services for people in all 50 states and United States territories. These federal services include our United States military—the army, navy, air force, marines, and coast guard. The federal government also prints money and postage stamps. It issues passports and makes sure that food and drugs are safe for people to use.

Choosing Leaders

The United States is a **democracy**, a government that is run by its people. As soon as you turn 18, you are to vote. You have a say in who runs the government.

Since the United States is so large, individuals do not run the country directly. Instead, the **citizens** elect representatives to pass laws in Congress. A citizen is a person who is born in a country or who has earned the right to become a member of that country by law. Citizens elect state

▲ Voting is every citizen's right and responsibility.

and local representatives, as well as the President, in national elections.

QUICK CHECK

Compare and Contrast **What is the difference between a citizen and a representative?**

115

Our national government, centered in Washington, D.C., has the same three branches that state governments have: executive, legislative, and judicial. Just like the branches of state government, each branch of the federal government has its own duties and responsibilities. Our national government also has a system of checks and balances so that one branch does not have too much power.

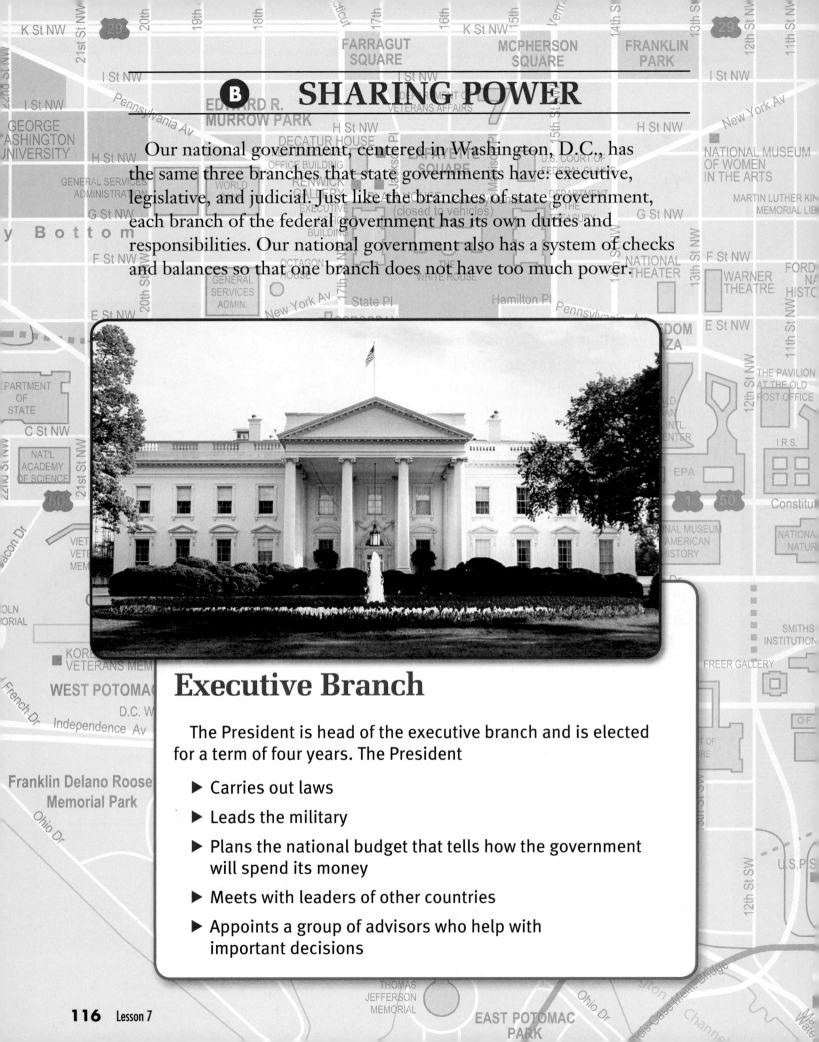

Executive Branch

The President is head of the executive branch and is elected for a term of four years. The President

▶ Carries out laws

▶ Leads the military

▶ Plans the national budget that tells how the government will spend its money

▶ Meets with leaders of other countries

▶ Appoints a group of advisors who help with important decisions

Legislative Branch

The legislative branch of the federal government is called the Congress. It has two parts, the Senate and the House of Representatives.

▶ The Senate has 100 senators, two from each state.

▶ The number of representatives in the House of Representatives depends on a state's population—the larger the population, the more representatives there will be in Congress.

Congress:

▶ Makes laws for our country

▶ Decides how much money to spend

Judicial Branch

The judicial branch of the federal government interprets the laws of our country.

▶ The Supreme Court is the highest court in the country.

▶ The federal judicial branch includes all the federal courts in the country.

QUICK CHECK

Summarize What does the judicial branch do?

Global Connections

The United Nations

After World War II ended, leaders from the United States and other powerful nations wanted to find a way to keep peace in the world. They formed the United Nations (UN). Member nations promise to work out their differences peacefully. The United States has been an important member of the UN from the beginning.

The UN also works to help children and to prevent and cure disease. The United Nations Children's Fund (UNICEF) is the branch of the UN that helps children around the world.

New York City

▲ The UN was formed in 1945 by 50 countries. Its headquarters is in New York City.

Sudan

This teacher from UNICEF works with 4th grade students in Sudan. ▶

ⓒ TRIBAL GOVERNMENT

In addition to local, state, and national governments, there are also tribal governments in the United States. Some Native American communities have tribal governments.

All Native Americans are citizens of the United States. They vote in local, state, and national elections, and follow United States law. However, many Native Americans live on **reservations**—land set aside for their use. These Native Americans are citizens of tribal governments. Most reservations are **sovereign**, or independent. Native Americans who live on reservations elect their own leaders and make their own laws. At the same time, they follow local, state, and national laws.

The Hopi Reservation in Arizona, for example, has a Hopi Tribal Council. This council takes care of reservation business and makes laws for the Hopi who live on the reservation. The council also works with other Native American groups, with the Arizona state government, and with the national government on issues that are important to the Hopi.

▲ This Hopi Tribal Council is trying to solve a disagreement among its members.

QUICK CHECK

Summarize What do tribal governments do?

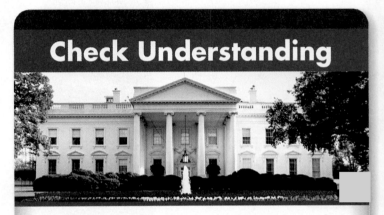

Check Understanding

1. **VOCABULARY** Write a paragraph about our national government using the following vocabulary words.
   federal   **democracy**   **citizen**

2. **READING SKILL Compare and Contrast** Use your diagram from page 114 to write about the differences between a tribal government and the national government.

 3. **Write About It** Write a paragraph about how the national government affects the people of the United States.

VOCABULARY

jury p. 121

patriotism p. 123

rule of law p. 124

justice p. 124

READING SKILL

Compare and Contrast
Copy the diagram below. FIll it in with facts about our rights and responsibilities.

Different   Alike   Different

STANDARDS FOCUS

SOCIAL STUDIES Civic Ideals and Practices

GEOGRAPHY Human Systems

OUR DEMOCRATIC VALUES

Statue of Liberty

Visual Preview

What democratic values do Americans share?

A The Declaration of Independence states that all people are created equal.

B Americans value diversity and work for the common good.

C Americans value truth, equality, justice, and the rule of law.

ⒶRIGHTS AND RESPONSIBILITIES

In 1776 people living in the American colonies decided they did not want to live under British rule any longer. They wrote a document called the Declaration of Independence. It told the world that the colonists had the right to break away from Great Britain.

The colonists knew they didn't want another government in which they didn't have a say. They asked Thomas Jefferson to write the Declaration of Independence. In it, he wrote that all people are "created equal" and share rights that no one can take from them. He said that it was the job of governments to protect these rights.

Three important rights that unite all Americans are "life, liberty, and the pursuit of happiness." *Life* means that we have the right to live free of violence. *Liberty* describes our right to act, speak, and think the way we please. The *pursuit of happiness* is the freedom to search for things that make us happy. Responsibilities accompany these rights.

Being a Responsible Citizen

One of our most important rights, the right to vote, is also an important responsibility. When we vote, we let our representatives and others know how we feel about things. Voters choose who will make our laws.

All men are created equal.
—THOMAS JEFFERSON

In addition to voting, all citizens are asked to pay taxes and follow laws. At times, citizens must serve on a **jury**. A jury is a group of citizens in a court of law who decide whether a person is innocent or guilty. By doing all these things and acting as a responsible citizen, Americans protect their rights and the rights of their family, community, state, and country.

QUICK CHECK

Compare and Contrast What is the difference between the rights and responsibilities of voting?

A group of people gathered in 1963 to hear Martin Luther King, Jr., give a speech about the rights of all Americans.

ⓑ WORKING TOGETHER

Not only do we have rights and responsibilities, but we have power as citizens. In lesson 6, you learned how a bill becomes a law. That's just one of the ways citizens work together to change things.

The Common Good

Americans also make changes by working for the common good—what is best for everyone. In 2005, for example, a company wanted to build a new store in a city in Oregon. People in the community worried that the store would create too much traffic and cause pollution of nearby streams. After many long discussions with the company, the community convinced it to build elsewhere. The community worked together for the common good and won!

Organizations also work for the common good. One example is the Red Cross. It works to help people in need in the United States and around the world.

Some people work for the common good by volunteering. When you volunteer, you help others without expecting anything in return. There are many ways to volunteer. Some

◀ These students show their patriotism by painting a flag.

people join the Peace Corps, a group of Americans who help people around the world. Others volunteer in their own communities.

Patriotism

Working toward the common good is also part of patriotism. **Patriotism** is the respect and loyal support of one's country. You show patriotism when you wave a flag, recite the Pledge of Allegiance, or sing the national anthem. You're also being patriotic when you step in to stop someone from being treated unfairly and when you tell the truth, especially when it's difficult.

Calvin Coolidge, President of the United States from 1923 to 1929, said:

"Patriotism is easy to understand in America; it means looking out for yourself by looking out for your country.**"**

QUICK CHECK

Main Idea and Details What are some ways you can show your patriotism?

Citizenship
Volunteering

When a tornado destroyed some houses in their town, Talia, Marcia, and Sandra wanted to help. They decided to volunteer at their local food bank. They helped pack boxes of personal care items, such as shampoo and soap. The boxes were then sent to the victims of the tornado.

Write About It Write a letter describing how you would help victims of a natural disaster such as a hurricane or tornado.

123

C   WHAT WE SHARE

As Americans and as patriots, we value our nation's diversity. People in our country are from many different races, cultures, and ethnic groups. People have come to the United States from every continent and from every country in the world. This is one of the things that makes our country special. Look at the pie chart below to see our nation's diversity.

Americans of every age, race, and ethnicity share similar values. ▼

Justice and the Rule of Law

In a country made up of different people with different ideas and goals, Americans sometimes disagree. When we do, we rely on laws for solutions. Americans believe in the **rule of law**. All of us, even the President, are ruled by our laws. Laws apply to all people equally. **Justice**, or fair treatment, is an important value in our laws. If Americans believe they have been treated unfairly, they can go to court and seek justice.

Truth is an American value, too, and an important part of our laws. We must tell the truth in court, so that no one goes to jail because of lies. We must tell the truth in business, so people are not cheated out of their money. Our government must also be truthful, so voters can make decisions based on facts they can trust.

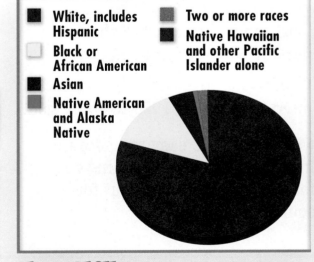

United States Cultural Groups, 2005

- ■ White, includes Hispanic
- ▢ Black or African American
- ■ Asian
- ▨ Native American and Alaska Native
- ▨ Two or more races
- ■ Native Hawaiian and other Pacific Islander alone

Chart Skill

What is the largest cultural group in the United States?

◀ Martin Luther King, Jr. and his wife Coretta Scott King, marching in Selma, Alabama, fought for fairness for Americans of all races.

Fighting for Fairness

Treating people equally is an American value. It's also stated in the Declaration of Independence. There have been many times in our history when some Americans were not treated fairly. Native Americans had land taken from them. Africans were brought here in slavery. German and Japanese Americans faced discrimination during the world wars.

Throughout our history, however, people have stood up to fight for equality. Responsible and patriotic Americans have demanded that our country live up to its values.

QUICK CHECK

Main Idea and Details Why is truth an important American value?

Check Understanding

1. **VOCABULARY** Write one sentence for each vocabulary word.
   justice   patriotism

2. **READING SKILL Compare and Contrast** Use your chart from page 120 to write a sentence about your responsibilities.

3. **Write About It** Write a paragraph about how people's idea of the common good might differ from place to place in our country.

125

Unit 2 Review and Assess

Vocabulary

Copy the sentences below. Use the list of vocabulary words to fill in the blanks.

region   precipitation

profit   interest

1. When banks lend money, they charge _____.

2. _____ is moisture that falls to the ground as rain, sleet, hail, or snow.

3. An area with common features is a _____.

4. _____ is money a business earns after it pays for all its costs.

Comprehension and Critical Thinking

5. What has caused erosion in the Appalachian Mountains?

6. Why does a bank charge interest on the money it lends?

7. **Critical Thinking** Why do state and local governments have different jobs and responsibilities?

8. **Reading Skill** What is the difference between weather and climate?

Skill

Use Line Graphs

Write a complete sentence to answer each question.

9. How has the population of Tennessee changed?

10. What year was the population of Tennessee the lowest?

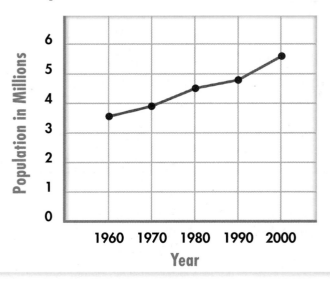

Population of Tennessee, 1960–2000

Test Preparation

Read the passage. Then answer the questions.

The United States is a large country, and one place in our country can be very different from another. For example, Florida has very different landforms and climate than Alaska. The two states also have different natural resources.

States that are near each other usually have a lot in common. Both Iowa and Nebraska are in the Great Plains. Arizona and New Mexico share desert areas. To help us understand our country more easily, we can divide states into regions. A region is an area with common features that set it apart from other areas. Regions are based on things such as shared landforms and climate.

1. What is the main idea of this passage?

   A. Iowa and Nebraska are neighbors.

   B. We divide our country into regions to make it easier to understand.

   C. The United States is a large country.

   D. Florida is warmer than Alaska.

2. Based on the passage, which conclusion can you draw?

   A. Florida and Alaska are in the same region.

   B. All states in the same region have desert areas.

   C. States that are in the same region usually have different climates.

   D. Arizona and New Mexico are probably in the same region.

3. What does the passage say about Florida and Alaska?

   A. The states have natural resources.

   B. Florida and Alaska have different resources, climate, and landforms.

   C. Florida and Alaska are states.

   D. The two states share landforms.

4. Describe why it might be important to protect the different landforms of the United States.

The Big Idea Activities

Write About the Big Idea

> How do people meet their needs?

Expository Essay

Use your Unit 2 foldable to help you write an essay. Answer the Big Idea question—How do people meet their needs? Write an essay about one of the regions of the United States. Your essay should answer the Big Idea question. You may choose to describe the region's geography, climate, and resources.

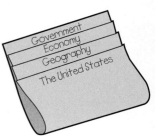

Travel Advertisement

Work in a small group to create a colorful and exciting brochure or poster for a region of the United States.

1. Each group should chose a region of the United States to promote.

2. Consider including information about the region's climate, natural resources, tourist attractions, cities, or national parks.

3. You may draw pictures or create a collage from newspapers or magazines.

4. Each member of the group should present some information about the region.

The Heartland of America, The Midwest

Reference Section

The Reference Section has many parts, each with a different type of information. Use this section to look up people, places, and events as you study.

Sequence Events

In this unit you will read about important events in United States history. When you read, think about the order in which events happen. This order is called the sequence of events. The sequence of events will help you understand and remember what you read.

Learn It

- Look for words such as *first, next, then, after, finally,* and *last*. These words show the order of events.

- Look for dates that tell you exactly when things happened. They are also clue words.

- Read the paragraph below. Look for the sequence of events.

Clue Words
These words show the sequence of events.

Events
These words describe each event.

About 20,000 years ago, during the last Ice Age, people traveled thousands of miles to get to North America looking for a better life. They became the first Native Americans. Much later, about 3,000 years ago, a culture, or way of life, began in the Ohio River Valley. These people traded and made crafts. Native Americans who lived along the coast depended on the ocean or rivers for food. While those who lived inland hunted and gathered berries and nuts from the forest. Today, Native Americans live throughout the United States.

Try It

Copy and complete the chart below. Then, fill in the chart by recording the events on page 8 in the correct sequence.

How did you figure out the sequence of events?

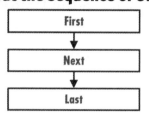

First
↓
Next
↓
Last

Apply It

- Review the sequencing steps in Learn It.

- Read the paragraph below. Then, create a sequence of events chart using the information.

In 1295, a man named Marco Polo returned to his home in Italy after a long journey in Asia. In 1447, thanks to a new way to print books, many Europeans read about Marco Polo's travels which described golden palaces, jewels, delicious spices, and other wonders.

In 1492, a man who had read the stories set out with three ships for Asia. Instead of sailing east, he sailed west. When he finally landed, he wasn't in Asia. He was on an island in the Caribbean Sea in North America.

Unit 2 • Reading Skills

Compare and Contrast

In this unit you will learn how geography affects how people live and work in the United States. Learning to compare and contrast will help you understand what you read about in social studies.

Learn It

- To compare two or more things, note how they are similar, or alike.
- To contrast two or more things, note how they are different.
- Read the passage. Think about how living in Gloucester, Massachusetts, and Tarpon Springs, Florida, are alike and different.

Similarities
People in both towns earn a living from the sea.

Differences
People earn a living by fishing in Gloucester.
In Tarpon Springs, they dive for sponges.

Gloucester, Massachusetts, is on the Atlantic Ocean. People there have always made a living from the sea. They fish for cod and trap lobsters. In summer, tourists visit the area's beaches or go whale watching.

Tarpon Springs, Florida, is on the Anconte River, near Florida's Gulf Coast. People in Tarpon Springs make a living from the sea, too, but instead of fishing, they dive for sponges. Tourists visit the docks to buy sponges and other souvenirs.

Similarities
Tourists visit both towns.

Try It

Copy and complete the Venn diagram to help you compare and contrast the information. Fill in the chart with details from the paragraphs on page R4.

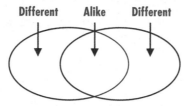

Different   Alike   Different

What information did you look for to compare and contrast?

Apply It

- Review the steps for comparing and contrasting in Learn It.

- Read the passage below. Then create a Venn diagram using the information.

Our changing economy has affected how and where people live. At one time, most people moved to rural areas. They needed lots of land because they worked in agriculture. Later people moved from rural areas to urban areas in order to find jobs in the manufacturing industry. Today many people live in urban areas.

Geography Handbook

Geography and You

Geography is the study of our Earth and the people who live here. Most people think of geography as learning about cities, states, and countries, but geography is more than that. Geography includes learning about land, such as plains and mountains. Geography also helps us learn how to use land and water wisely.

Did you know that people are part of geography? Geography includes the study of how people adapt to live in a new place. How people move around, how they move goods, and how ideas travel from place to place are also parts of geography.

In fact, geography includes so many things that geographers have divided this information into six elements, or ideas, so you can better understand them.

Six Essential Elements

The World in Spatial Terms: Where is a place located, and what land or water features does this place have?

Places and Regions: What is special about a place, and what makes it different from other places?

Physical Systems: What has shaped the land and climate of a place, and how does this affect the plants, animals, and people there?

Human Systems: How do people, ideas, and goods move from place to place?

Environment and Society: How have people changed the land and water of a place, and how have the land and water affected the people of a place?

Uses of Geography: How does geography influence events in the past, present, and the future?

Five Themes of Geography

You have read about the six elements of geography. The five themes of geography are another way of dividing the ideas of geography. The themes, or topics, are **location**, **place**, **region**, **movement**, and **human interaction**. Using these five themes is another way to understand events you read about in this book.

1. Location

Washington, D. C.

In geography, *location* means an exact spot on the planet. A location is usually a street name and number. You write a location when you address a letter.

2. Place

Seattle, Washington

A *place* is described by its physical features, such as rivers, mountains, or valleys. You would also include the human features, such as cities, language, and traditions, in the description of a place.

3. Region

Florida Everglades National Park

A *region* is a larger area than a place or location. The people in a region are affected by landforms. Their region has typical jobs and customs. For example, the fertile soil of the Mississippi Lowlands helps farmers in the region grow crops.

4. Movement

Los Angeles, California

Throughout history, people have *moved* to find better land or a better life. Geographers study why these movements occurred. They also study how people's movements have changed a region.

5. Human Interaction

Pittsburgh, Pennsylvania

Geographers are interested in how people adapt to their environment. Geographers also study how people change their environment. This *interaction* between people and their environments determines how land is used for cities, farms, or parks.

Dictionary of Geographic Terms

1 BASIN A bowl-shaped landform surrounded by higher land

2 BAY Part of an ocean or lake that extends deeply into the land

3 CANAL A channel built to carry water for irrigation or transportation

4 CANYON A deep, narrow valley with steep sides

5 COAST The land along an ocean

6 DAM A wall built across a river, creating a lake that stores water

7 DELTA Land made of soil left behind as a river drains into a larger body of water

8 DESERT A dry environment with few plants and animals

9 FAULT The border between two of the plates that make up Earth's crust

10 GLACIER A huge sheet of ice that moves slowly across the land

11 GULF Part of an ocean that extends into the land; larger than a bay

12 HARBOR A sheltered place along a coast where boats dock safely

13 HILL A rounded, raised landform; not as high as a mountain

14 ISLAND A body of land completely surrounded by water

15 LAKE A body of water completely surrounded by land

16 MESA A hill with a flat top; smaller than a plateau

17 **MOUNTAIN** A high landform with steep sides; higher than a hill

18 **MOUNTAIN PASS** A narrow gap through a mountain range

19 **MOUTH** The place where a river empties into a larger body of water

20 **OCEAN** A large body of salt water; oceans cover much of Earth's surface

21 **PENINSULA** A body of land nearly surrounded by water

22 **PLAIN** A large area of nearly flat land

23 **PLATEAU** A high, flat area that rises steeply above the surrounding land

24 **PORT** A place where ships load and unload their goods

25 **RESERVOIR** A natural or artificial lake used to store water

26 **RIVER** A stream of water that flows across the land and empties into another body of water

27 **SOURCE** The starting point of a river

28 **VALLEY** An area of low land between hills or mountains

29 **VOLCANO** An opening in Earth's surface through which hot rock and ash are forced out

30 **WATERFALL** A flow of water falling vertically

Reviewing Geography Skills

Read a Physical Map

Maps are drawings of places on Earth. Most maps use colors and symbols to show information. Physical maps show and label landforms, such as mountains and deserts, and water features, such as lakes and rivers. Map makers use shading and color to show different physical features, such as blue to show water or dark shading to show mountains.

Map Title Map titles tell you what information is on the map.

Inset Map An inset map is a small map set into the main map. It shows an area that is too large, too small, or too far away to be included on the main map. Inset maps usually use a different scale than the main map.

Map Key The map key, or legend, gives the meaning of the colors and symbols on a map.

Map Scale The map scale is a line that shows the relationship between distances on a map and distances on Earth. Here, the length of the line on the map represents 400 miles on Earth.

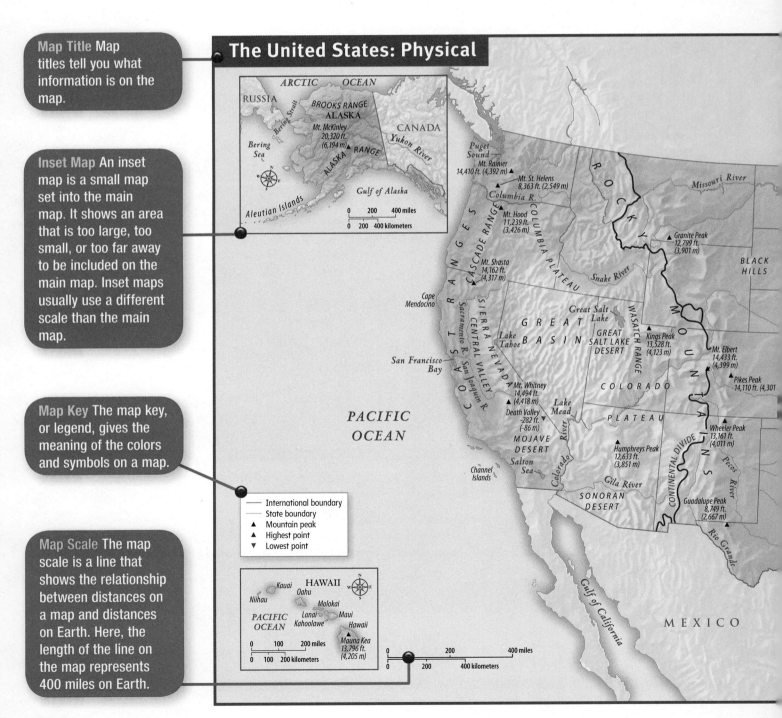

The United States: Physical

ARCTIC OCEAN
RUSSIA
BROOKS RANGE
ALASKA
Bering Strait
Mt. McKinley 20,320 ft. (6,194 m)
CANADA
Bering Sea
ALASKA RANGE
Yukon River
Gulf of Alaska
Aleutian Islands
0 200 400 miles
0 200 400 kilometers

Puget Sound
Mt. Rainier 14,410 ft. (4,392 m)
Mt. St. Helens 8,363 ft. (2,549 m)
Columbia R.
Mt. Hood 11,239 ft. (3,426 m)
ROCKY
Missouri River
Granite Peak 12,799 ft. (3,901 m)
BLACK HILLS
Mt. Shasta 14,162 ft. (4,317 m)
COLUMBIA PLATEAU
Snake River
CASCADE RANGE
COAST RANGES
Cape Mendocino
Sacramento R.
CENTRAL VALLEY
SIERRA NEVADA
Great Salt Lake
GREAT BASIN
GREAT SALT LAKE DESERT
WASATCH RANGE
Kings Peak 13,528 ft. (4,123 m)
MOUNTAINS
Mt. Elbert 14,433 ft. (4,399 m)
Pikes Peak 14,110 ft. (4,301
Lake Tahoe
San Francisco Bay
San Joaquin R.
Mt. Whitney 14,494 ft. (4,418 m)
Death Valley -282 ft. (-86 m)
Lake Mead
COLORADO PLATEAU
CONTINENTAL DIVIDE
Wheeler Peak 13,161 ft. (4,011 m)
PACIFIC OCEAN
Humphreys Peak 12,633 ft. (3,851 m)
MOJAVE DESERT
Colorado River
Salton Sea
Channel Islands
Gila River
SONORAN DESERT
Guadalupe Peak 8,749 ft. (2,667 m)
Pecos River
Rio Grande
Gulf of California
MEXICO

International boundary
State boundary
▲ Mountain peak
▲ Highest point
▼ Lowest point

HAWAII
Kauai
Oahu
Niihau
Molokai
PACIFIC OCEAN
Lanai
Kahoolawe
Maui
Hawaii
Mauna Kea 13,796 ft. (4,205 m)
0 100 200 miles
0 100 200 kilometers

0 200 400 miles
0 200 400 kilometers

Think About It About how far is it from Mt. Hood to Mt. Shasta in the Cascade Range?

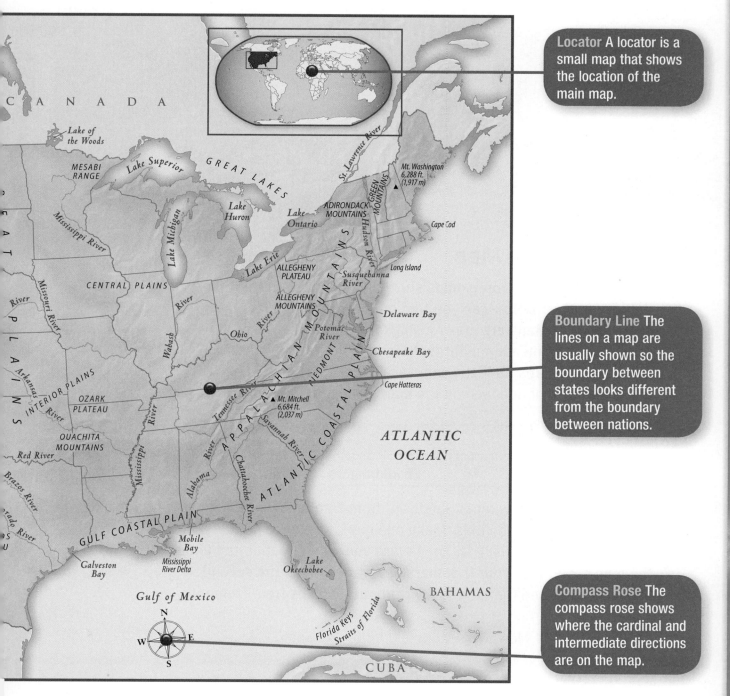

Locator A locator is a small map that shows the location of the main map.

Boundary Line The lines on a map are usually shown so the boundary between states looks different from the boundary between nations.

Compass Rose The compass rose shows where the cardinal and intermediate directions are on the map.

CANADA

Lake of the Woods

MESABI RANGE

Lake Superior

GREAT LAKES

St. Lawrence River

GREEN MOUNTAINS

Mt. Washington 6,288 ft. (1,917 m)

Mississippi River

Lake Michigan

Lake Huron

Lake Ontario

ADIRONDACK MOUNTAINS

Hudson River

Cape Cod

GREAT PLAINS

CENTRAL PLAINS

Lake Erie

ALLEGHENY PLATEAU

ALLEGHENY MOUNTAINS

Susquehanna River

Long Island

Missouri River

River

APPALACHIAN MOUNTAINS

Delaware Bay

Ohio River

Potomac River

PIEDMONT

Chesapeake Bay

Wabash

INTERIOR PLAINS

Arkansas River

OZARK PLATEAU

Tennessee River

Mt. Mitchell 6,684 ft. (2,037 m)

Cape Hatteras

ATLANTIC OCEAN

Red River

OUACHITA MOUNTAINS

Mississippi River

Alabama River

Savannah River

ATLANTIC COASTAL PLAIN

Brazos River

Chattahoochee River

Colorado River

GULF COASTAL PLAIN

Mobile Bay

Lake Okeechobee

BAHAMAS

Galveston Bay

Mississippi River Delta

Gulf of Mexico

Florida Keys

Straits of Florida

CUBA

N
W E
S

GH7

Read a Route Map

You know that many route maps show distances as shorter than they are on Earth. How can you find out how much shorter the distances are? Maps are drawn using map scales. A map scale shows a unit of measurement that stands for a real distance on Earth. Not all maps have the same scale. You can see on page GH9 that a distance of one inch on the map equals 50 miles on Earth.

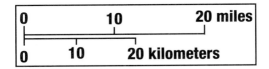

Look at the map. How far is Sandusky from Fremont? Place a slip of paper just below both cities. Make one mark where Fremont is and another where Sandusky is. Then place your slip of paper just under the map scale, with your first mark at zero. Where is the second mark? You can see that Sandusky is about 25 miles from Fremont.

Think About It How far is Mansfield from Oberlin?

Route Maps

Suppose you want to go somewhere you have never been before. How would you know which roads to take? You would use a route map. Route maps show the roads in a certain area. By reading a route map, you can figure out how to get from one place to another. Many route maps are also grid maps, like this one.

Grid Maps

A grid map has a special grid to help you locate things. Each box can be named with a number and a letter. For example, you might want to find Akron, Ohio, but you don't know where to look. You can see from the index that Akron is located in square B-3. Put one finger on the letter B along the side of the map. Put another finger on the number 3 at the top. Then move your fingers across and down the map until they meet. You have found B-3 on the grid, and now that you only have to search one square instead of the whole map, it's easy to find Akron.

Think About It Find Lima on the map. What grid box is it in?

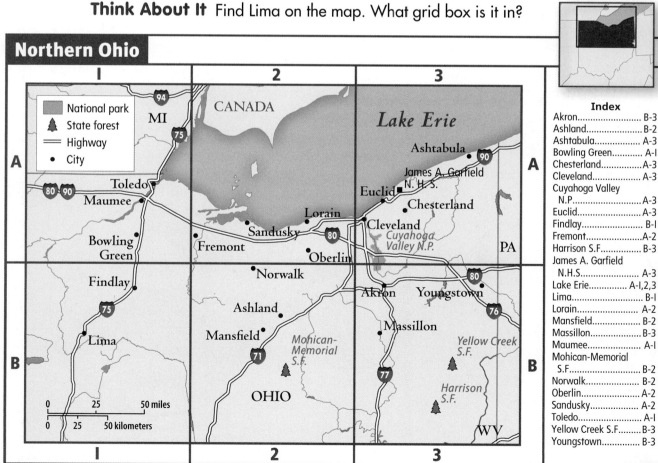

Northern Ohio

	Index	
	Akron	B-3
	Ashland	B-2
	Ashtabula	A-3
	Bowling Green	A-1
	Chesterland	A-3
	Cleveland	A-3
	Cuyahoga Valley N.P.	A-3
	Euclid	A-3
	Findlay	B-1
	Fremont	A-2
	Harrison S.F.	B-3
	James A. Garfield N.H.S.	A-3
	Lake Erie	A-1,2,3
	Lima	B-1
	Lorain	A-2
	Mansfield	B-2
	Massillon	B-3
	Maumee	A-1
	Mohican-Memorial S.F.	B-2
	Norwalk	B-2
	Oberlin	A-2
	Sandusky	A-2
	Toledo	A-1
	Yellow Creek S.F.	B-3
	Youngstown	B-3

Hemispheres

You can think of Earth as a sphere, like a ball or a globe. A hemisphere is half of a sphere. Geographers have divided Earth into the Northern Hemisphere and the Southern Hemisphere at the equator, an imaginary line that circles Earth halfway between the North Pole and the South Pole. Another important imaginary line is the prime meridian. It divides Earth from east to west. The area west of the prime meridian is called the Western Hemisphere, and the area east of the prime meridian is called the Eastern Hemisphere.

Think About It In which two hemispheres is North America?

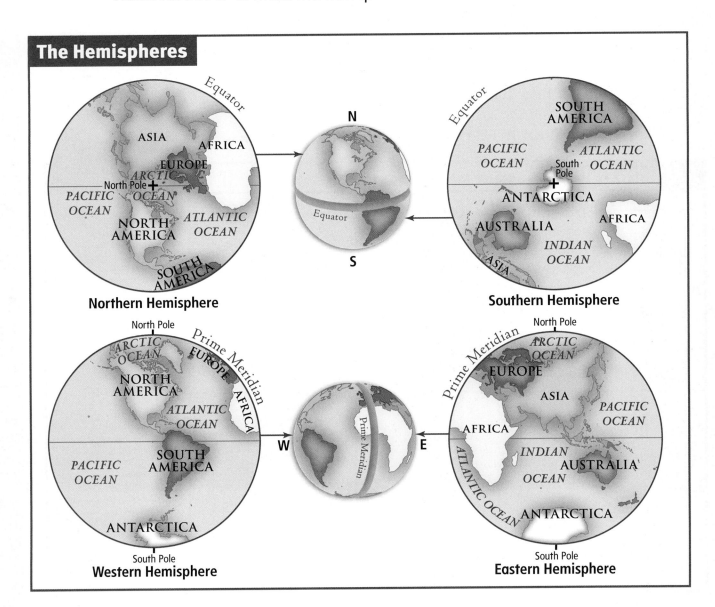

The Hemispheres

Northern Hemisphere

Southern Hemisphere

Western Hemisphere

Eastern Hemisphere

Latitude and Longitude

Earth can be divided into a grid of lines called latitude and longitude. Lines of latitude measure how far north or south a place is from the equator. Lines of longitude measure distance east or west from the prime meridian. Both the equator and the prime meridian represent 0 degrees. The symbol for degrees is °. Latitude lines measure the distance in degrees from the equator, and longitude lines measure the distance in degrees from the prime meridian. Look at the map. You can see that Los Angeles is located very near the longitude line labeled 120°W at the top of the map. That means that Los Angeles is about 120° west of the prime meridian.

Think About It Is Lagos north or south of the equator?

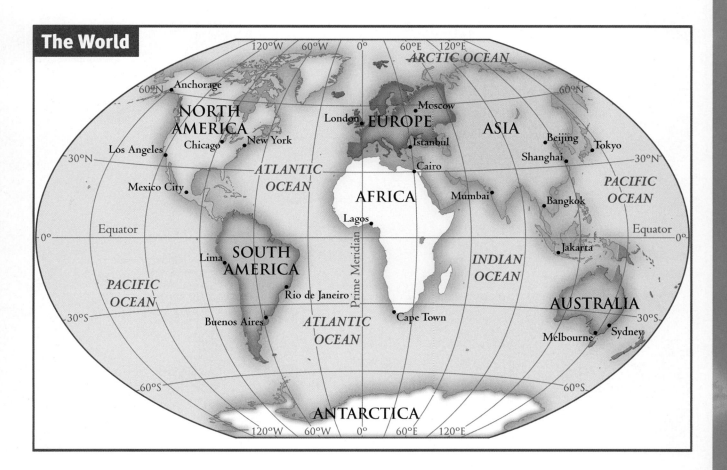

ARCTIC OCEAN
180°W   70°N   120°W
RUSSIA
Arctic Circle
CANADA
Nome   Yukon R.   Fairbanks
ALASKA
60°N
Anchorage
130°W
Juneau
0   200   400 miles
0   200   400 kilometers
170°W   160°W   150°W   140°W
40°N   130°W

Seattle
Olympia   Spokane   River   Great Falls   Missouri River
WASHINGTON   Helena   MONTANA
Columbia
Portland   Billings
Salem
Eugene   IDAHO
OREGON   Boise   WYOMING
Snake River   Casper
Eureka   Pocatello
Redding   Great Salt Lake   Ogden   Cheyenne
Reno   Salt Lake City   Provo
Sacramento   Carson City   Denver
San Francisco   NEVADA   UTAH   COLORADO
Oakland   Colorado Springs
San Jose   Colorado River   Pueblo
Fresno
CALIFORNIA   Las Vegas
Bakersfield   Santa Fe
PACIFIC OCEAN   Albuquerque
Los Angeles   ARIZONA   NEW MEXICO
Long Beach   Phoenix
30°N   San Diego   Rio Grande
Tucson
El Paso

Gulf of California

0   200   400 miles
0   200   400 kilometers
130°W

160°W   HAWAII   155°W
Kauai
Oahu
Niihau   Molokai
Honolulu   Maui
PACIFIC   Lanai
OCEAN   Kahoolawe   20°N
Hilo
Hawaii
0   100   200 miles
0   100   200 kilometers

MEXICO

____ International boundary
____ State boundary
⊛ National capital
★ State capital
• Other city

Tropic of Cancer
120°W   110°W
20°N

CANADA

NORTH
DAKOTA Grand
        Forks
Fargo
Bismarck MINNESOTA Duluth Marquette

SOUTH
DAKOTA St. Paul
Pierre Minneapolis Green
               Bay WISCONSIN
Sioux
Falls Milwaukee
       Madison

NEBRASKA Cedar
          Rapids IOWA
Omaha Des
       Moines
Lincoln

Lake Superior

MICHIGAN Lake
          Huron

Lake Michigan Grand
               Rapids
Lansing Detroit

Chicago Lake Erie
Gary Toledo Cleveland

Davenport OHIO
ILLINOIS INDIANA Columbus Pittsburgh

NEW
HAMPSHIRE MAINE
VERMONT Augusta
Montpelier Portland
           Concord
           Boston
Albany MASSACHUSETTS
NEW YORK Providence
Buffalo Hartford RHODE ISLAND
        CONNECTICUT
Newark New York
PENNSYLVANIA Trenton NEW JERSEY
Harrisburg Philadelphia
Baltimore Dover
           DELAWARE

Lake Ontario

Kansas
City Topeka
KANSAS Kansas
        City
Wichita

Jefferson
City St. Louis Springfield Indianapolis
MISSOURI Evansville

Washington, D.C. Annapolis
WEST MARYLAND
VIRGINIA
Charleston Richmond
Cincinnati VIRGINIA Norfolk
Frankfort Louisville
KENTUCKY

Tulsa
Oklahoma
City OKLAHOMA
Fort
Smith ARKANSAS
Little
Rock

Nashville
TENNESSEE Tennessee River Knoxville
Memphis

NORTH
CAROLINA Raleigh
Charlotte
Columbia
SOUTH CAROLINA

ATLANTIC
OCEAN

Fort
Worth Dallas
TEXAS
San Antonio
Corpus
Christi
Laredo

Red River
Shreveport
LOUISIANA
Baton Rouge
Austin Houston
New Orleans

Birmingham
MISSISSIPPI ALABAMA
Jackson
Montgomery
Mobile
Biloxi

Atlanta
GEORGIA
Columbus
Charleston
Savannah

Tallahassee
Jacksonville

Gulf of Mexico

Orlando
FLORIDA
Tampa
Lake Okeechobee

Miami

BAHAMAS

CUBA

N
W E
S

Platte River
Missouri River
Arkansas River
Oklahoma River
Mississippi River
Ohio River
Brazos River
Colorado River

GH13

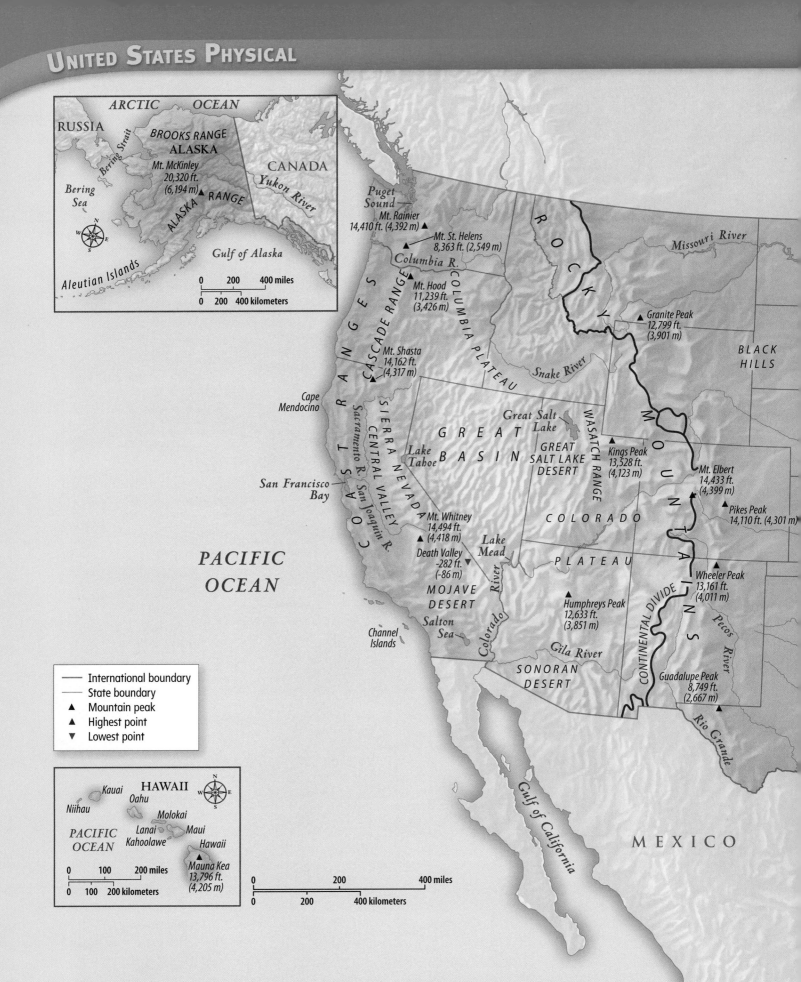

ARCTIC OCEAN

RUSSIA

BROOKS RANGE
ALASKA

Bering Strait

Mt. McKinley
20,320 ft.
(6,194 m)

CANADA
Yukon River

ALASKA RANGE

Bering Sea

Gulf of Alaska

Aleutian Islands

0   200   400 miles
0   200   400 kilometers

PACIFIC OCEAN

Puget Sound
Mt. Rainier
14,410 ft. (4,392 m)

Mt. St. Helens
8,363 ft. (2,549 m)

Columbia R.

Mt. Hood
11,239 ft.
(3,426 m)

CASCADE RANGE

COLUMBIA PLATEAU

ROCKY

Missouri River

Mt. Shasta
14,162 ft.
(4,317 m)

Snake River

Granite Peak
12,799 ft.
(3,901 m)

BLACK HILLS

Cape Mendocino

COAST RANGES

Sacramento R.

SIERRA NEVADA

CENTRAL VALLEY

Lake Tahoe

GREAT BASIN

Great Salt Lake

WASATCH RANGE

GREAT SALT LAKE DESERT

Kings Peak
13,528 ft.
(4,123 m)

MOUNTAINS

Mt. Elbert
14,433 ft.
(4,399 m)

Pikes Peak
14,110 ft. (4,301 m)

San Francisco Bay

San Joaquin R.

Mt. Whitney
14,494 ft.
(4,418 m)

Death Valley
-282 ft.
(-86 m)

Lake Mead

COLORADO

PLATEAU

Wheeler Peak
13,161 ft.
(4,011 m)

PACIFIC OCEAN

Channel Islands

MOJAVE DESERT

Salton Sea

Colorado River

Humphreys Peak
12,633 ft.
(3,851 m)

CONTINENTAL DIVIDE

Pecos River

SONORAN DESERT

Gila River

Guadalupe Peak
8,749 ft.
(2,667 m)

Rio Grande

— International boundary
— State boundary
▲ Mountain peak
▲ Highest point
▼ Lowest point

Gulf of California

MEXICO

HAWAII

Kauai
Oahu
Niihau
Molokai
PACIFIC OCEAN
Lanai   Maui
Kahoolawe   Hawaii
Mauna Kea
13,796 ft.
(4,205 m)

0   100   200 miles
0   100   200 kilometers

0   200   400 miles
0   200   400 kilometers

CANADA

Lake of
the Woods

MESABI
RANGE

Lake Superior

GREAT LAKES

St. Lawrence River

Mt. Washington
6,288 ft.
(1,917 m) ▲

GREEN
MOUNTAINS

Lake
Huron

ADIRONDACK
MOUNTAINS

Cape Cod

Lake Michigan

Lake
Ontario

Mississippi River

Hudson River

Missouri River

CENTRAL PLAINS

Lake Erie

ALLEGHENY
PLATEAU

Susquehanna
River

Long Island

Platte   River

Wabash

River

Ohio

ALLEGHENY
MOUNTAINS

APPALACHIAN

River

Delaware Bay

River

Potomac
River

Chesapeake Bay

GREAT   PLAINS

Arkansas

INTERIOR PLAINS

OZARK
PLATEAU

River

Mississippi River

MOUNTAINS

PIEDMONT

Cape Hatteras

Tennessee River

Mt. Mitchell
6,684 ft.
(2,037 m) ▲

River

OUACHITA
MOUNTAINS

Red River

ATLANTIC COASTAL PLAIN

Savannah River

ATLANTIC
OCEAN

Alabama

Brazos River

River

Chattahoochee River

Colorado River

EDWARDS
PLATEAU

GULF COASTAL PLAIN

Mobile
Bay

Lake
Okeechobee

Galveston
Bay

Mississippi
River Delta

BAHAMAS

Gulf of Mexico

N

W   E

Florida Keys

Straits of Florida

S

CUBA

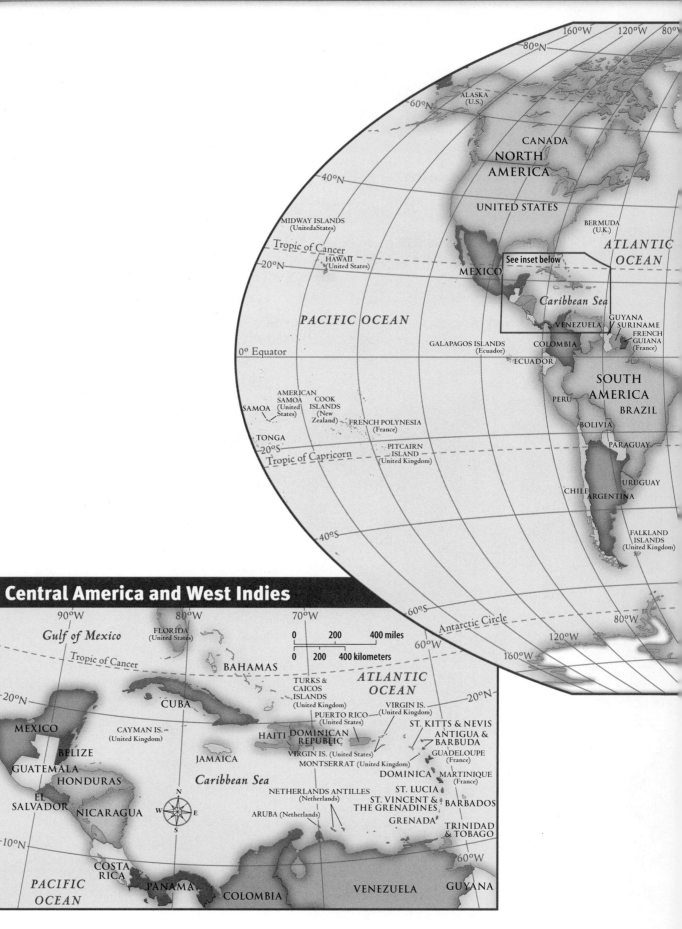

160°W 120°W 80°

80°N

60°N

ALASKA
(U.S.)

40°N

CANADA
NORTH
AMERICA

UNITED STATES

MIDWAY ISLANDS
(UnitedaStates)

BERMUDA
(U.K.)

ATLANTIC
OCEAN

Tropic of Cancer

20°N

HAWAII
(United States)

MEXICO

See inset below

Caribbean Sea

PACIFIC OCEAN

VENEZUELA

GUYANA
SURINAME
FRENCH
GUIANA
(France)

GALAPAGOS ISLANDS
(Ecuador)

COLOMBIA

0° Equator

ECUADOR

SOUTH
AMERICA

AMERICAN
SAMOA
(United
States)

COOK
ISLANDS
(New
Zealand)

PERU

BRAZIL

SAMOA

FRENCH POLYNESIA
(France)

TONGA

BOLIVIA

PITCAIRN
ISLAND
(United Kingdom)

PARAGUAY

20°S

Tropic of Capricorn

CHILE

URUGUAY

ARGENTINA

40°S

FALKLAND
ISLANDS
(United Kingdom)

60°S

Antarctic Circle

60°W

120°W

80°W

160°W

Central America and West Indies

90°W 80°W 70°W

Gulf of Mexico

FLORIDA
(United States)

0   200   400 miles

0   200   400 kilometers

ATLANTIC
OCEAN

Tropic of Cancer

BAHAMAS

60°W

20°N

CUBA

TURKS &
CAICOS
ISLANDS
(United Kingdom)

VIRGIN IS.
(United Kingdom)

20°N

MEXICO

CAYMAN IS.
(United Kingdom)

PUERTO RICO
(United States)

ST. KITTS & NEVIS

BELIZE

HAITI

DOMINICAN
REPUBLIC

ANTIGUA &
BARBUDA

GUATEMALA

JAMAICA

VIRGIN IS. (United States)

GUADELOUPE
(France)

HONDURAS

MONTSERRAT (United Kingdom)

DOMINICA

MARTINIQUE
(France)

EL
SALVADOR

NICARAGUA

Caribbean Sea

N

W   E

S

NETHERLANDS ANTILLES
(Netherlands)

ST. LUCIA

ST. VINCENT &
THE GRENADINES

BARBADOS

10°N

ARUBA (Netherlands)

GRENADA

TRINIDAD
& TOBAGO

60°W

COSTA
RICA

PACIFIC
OCEAN

PANAMA

COLOMBIA

VENEZUELA

GUYANA

GH16

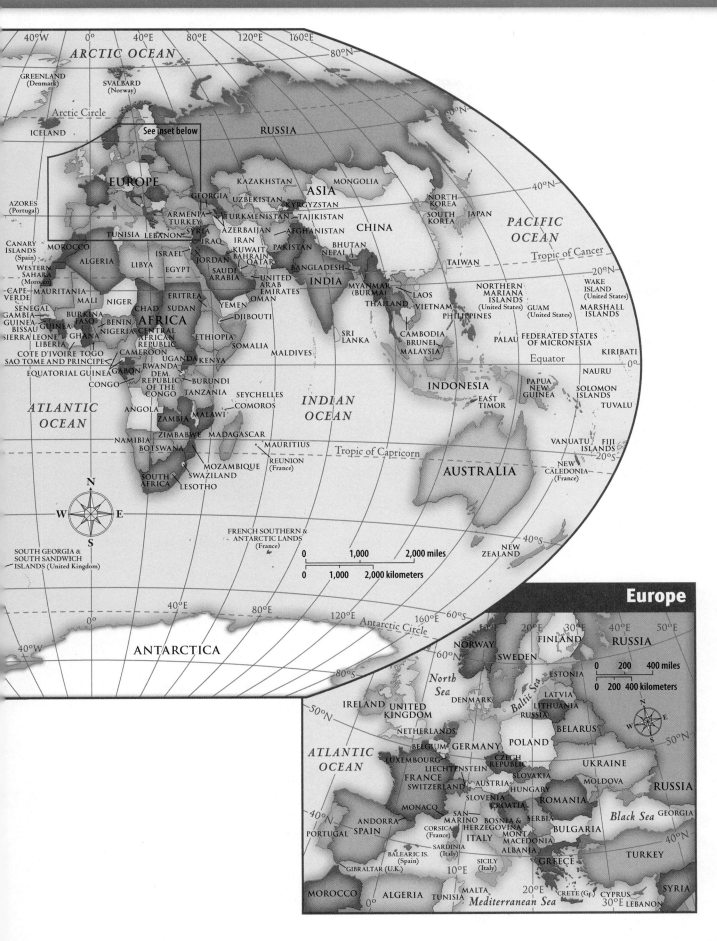

ARCTIC OCEAN

40°W 0° 40°E 80°E 120°E 160°E

80°N

GREENLAND
(Denmark)

SVALBARD
(Norway)

Arctic Circle

ICELAND

See inset below

RUSSIA

60°N

EUROPE

KAZAKHSTAN

MONGOLIA

ASIA

40°N

AZORES
(Portugal)

GEORGIA

UZBEKISTAN

KYRGYZSTAN

NORTH
KOREA

ARMENIA
TURKEY

TURKMENISTAN

TAJIKISTAN

SOUTH
KOREA

JAPAN

PACIFIC
OCEAN

TUNISIA LEBANON

SYRIA

AZERBAIJAN

AFGHANISTAN

CHINA

CANARY
ISLANDS
(Spain)

MOROCCO

IRAQ

IRAN

PAKISTAN

BHUTAN

TAIWAN

Tropic of Cancer

ALGERIA

ISRAEL

KUWAIT
JORDAN BAHRAIN
QATAR

NEPAL

20°N

WESTERN
SAHARA
(Morocco)

LIBYA

EGYPT

SAUDI
ARABIA

UNITED
ARAB
EMIRATES

BANGLADESH

INDIA

MYANMAR
(BURMA)

LAOS

NORTHERN
MARIANA
ISLANDS
(United States)

WAKE
ISLAND
(United States)

CAPE
VERDE

MAURITANIA

MALI

NIGER

CHAD SUDAN

ERITREA

YEMEN

OMAN

THAILAND

VIETNAM

GUAM
(United States)

MARSHALL
ISLANDS

SENEGAL
GAMBIA
GUINEA
BISSAU
SIERRA LEONE

BURKINA
FASO

AFRICA

BENIN

NIGERIA

CENTRAL
AFRICAN
REPUBLIC

DJIBOUTI

ETHIOPIA

SRI
LANKA

CAMBODIA
BRUNEI
MALAYSIA

PHILIPPINES

PALAU

FEDERATED STATES
OF MICRONESIA

KIRIBATI

GUINEA
GHANA
LIBERIA

COTE D'IVOIRE TOGO
SAO TOME AND PRINCIPE

CAMEROON

UGANDA KENYA

SOMALIA

MALDIVES

Equator

NAURU

EQUATORIAL GUINEA

GABON

RWANDA
DEM.
REPUBLIC
OF THE
CONGO

BURUNDI

INDONESIA

PAPUA
NEW
GUINEA

SOLOMON
ISLANDS

CONGO

TANZANIA

SEYCHELLES

INDIAN
OCEAN

EAST
TIMOR

TUVALU

ATLANTIC
OCEAN

ANGOLA

ZAMBIA

COMOROS

MALAWI

ZIMBABWE MADAGASCAR

NAMIBIA
BOTSWANA

MAURITIUS

Tropic of Capricorn

VANUATU FIJI
ISLANDS

20°S

SOUTH
AFRICA

MOZAMBIQUE

SWAZILAND
LESOTHO

REUNION
(France)

AUSTRALIA

NEW
CALEDONIA
(France)

N
W   E
S

SOUTH GEORGIA &
SOUTH SANDWICH
ISLANDS (United Kingdom)

FRENCH SOUTHERN &
ANTARCTIC LANDS
(France)

0   1,000   2,000 miles

0   1,000   2,000 kilometers

40°S

NEW
ZEALAND

40°W

0°

40°E

80°E

120°E

160°E

60°S

Antarctic Circle

80°S

ANTARCTICA

Europe

20°E 30°E 40°E 50°E

FINLAND RUSSIA

NORWAY

SWEDEN

60°N

0   200   400 miles

0   200   400 kilometers

North
Sea

ESTONIA

Baltic Sea

LATVIA

IRELAND UNITED
KINGDOM

50°N

DENMARK

LITHUANIA

RUSSIA

BELARUS

N
W   E
S

50°N

NETHERLANDS

ATLANTIC
OCEAN

BELGIUM GERMANY

POLAND

UKRAINE

LUXEMBOURG
LIECHTENSTEIN

CZECH
REPUBLIC

SLOVAKIA

MOLDOVA

FRANCE
SWITZERLAND

AUSTRIA

HUNGARY

RUSSIA

40°N

SLOVENIA

ROMANIA

Black Sea

GEORGIA

MONACO

CROATIA

ANDORRA

SAN
MARINO

BOSNIA &
HERZEGOVINA

SERBIA

BULGARIA

40°N

PORTUGAL

SPAIN

CORSICA
(France)

MONT.
MACEDONIA

TURKEY

BALEARIC IS.
(Spain)

SARDINIA
(Italy)

ITALY

ALBANIA

GREECE

GIBRALTAR (U.K.)

10°E

SICILY
(Italy)

MOROCCO

ALGERIA

TUNISIA

MALTA

20°E

CRETE (Gr.)

CYPRUS

SYRIA

Mediterranean Sea

30°E LEBANON

0°

ARCTIC OCEAN

EUROPE

ASIA

ICELAND

Greenland Sea

Gunnbjorn 12,139 ft. (3,700 m) ▲

Oodaaq Island

Lincoln Sea

Queen Elizabeth Islands

Ellesmere Island

HAYES PENINSULA

Greenland

Chukchi Sea

Point Barrow

NORTH SLOPE

Beaufort Sea

Banks Island

Melville Island

Devon Island

Somerset

Prince of Wales I.

Victoria Island

Baffin Bay

Davis Strait

Arctic Circle

Cape Farewell

Bering Sea

Bering Strait

SEWARD PENINSULA

BROOKS RANGE

Mt. McKinley 20,320 ft. (6,194 m) ▲ ALASKA

ALASKA RANGE

Yukon R.

Baffin Island

BOOTHIA PENINSULA

MELVILLE PEN.

Foxe Basin

Labrador Sea

KENAI PENINSULA

Kodiak Island

Gulf of Alaska

Mt. Logan 19,551 ft. (5,959 m) ▲

MACKENZIE MTS.

Mackenzie R.

YUKON PLATEAU

Great Bear Lake

Great Slave Lake

Southampton Island

Hudson Strait

Ungava Bay

ALEXANDER ARCHIPELAGO

Queen Charlotte Islands

CANADA

Slave R.

Peace R.

Athabasca R.

Hudson Bay

Belcher Islands

Island of Newfoundland

AVALON PENINSULA

FRASER PLATEAU

COLUMBIA MTS.

Lake Athabasca

Churchill R.

CANADIAN SHIELD

James Bay

LAURENTIAN MTS.

Gulf of St. Lawrence

Cape Breton Island

Vancouver Island

COAST MOUNTAINS

COLUMBIA PLATEAU

Saskatchewan R.

ROCKY MOUNTAINS

Lake Winnipeg

GREAT MOUNTAINS

St. Lawrence R.

GASPE PEN.

Prince Edward Island

Nova Scotia

OLYMPIC PENINSULA

CASCADE RANGE

Snake R.

Great Salt Lake

Missouri River

Lake Superior

Ottawa ✪

Lake Huron

Lake Ontario

Gulf of Maine

Bay of Fundy

Cape Mendocino

COAST RANGES

SIERRA NEVADA

GREAT BASIN

COLORADO PLATEAU

HIGH PLAINS

Platte R.

Lake Michigan

CENTRAL LOWLAND

Lake Erie

APPALACHIAN MOUNTAINS

Cape Cod

Long Island

ATLANTIC OCEAN

Mt. Whitney 14,494 ft. (4,418 m) ▲

UNITED STATES

Arkansas River

OZARK PLATEAU

Ohio R.

Washington, D.C. ✪

Chesapeake Bay

Cape Hatteras

Death Valley —282 ft. (-86 m)

Colorado R.

Grand Canyon

Mississippi R.

Bermuda (U.K.)

Channel Islands

SONORAN DESERT

Red River

COASTAL PLAIN

PACIFIC OCEAN

BAJA CALIFORNIA

Rio Grande

Gulf of California

SIERRA MADRE OCCIDENTAL

MEXICO

SIERRA MADRE ORIENTAL

Gulf of Mexico

Tropic of Cancer

Florida Keys

BAHAMAS

Nassau ✪

DOMINICAN REPUBLIC

Tropic of Cancer

Havana ✪

CUBA

WEST INDIES

Hispaniola

Virgin Islands

Orizaba 18,855 ft. (5,747 m) ▲

YUCATÁN PENINSULA

Cozumel Island

Cayman Islands (U.K.)

HAITI

Port-au-Prince ✪

Santo Domingo

Guadeloupe

Martinique

Puerto Rico (U.S.)

México City ✪

GUATEMALA

BELIZE

Belmopan ✪

Kingston ✪

JAMAICA

TRINIDAD & TOBAGO

Port-of-Spain ✪

Isthmus of Tehuantepec

Guatemala City ✪

HONDURAS

Tegucigalpa ✪

Caribbean Sea

San Salvador ✪

EL SALVADOR

NICARAGUA

Lake Nicaragua

Managua ✪

COSTA RICA

Isthmus of Panama

Panamá ✪

SOUTH AMERICA

San José ✪

PANAMA

CENTRAL AMERICA

Legend:
— International boundary
✪ National capital
▲ Mountain peak

N
W E
S

| 0 | 300 | 600 miles |
| 0 | 300 | 600 kilometers |

Glossary

This glossary will help you to pronounce and understand the meanings of the vocabulary in this book. The page number at the end of the definition tells you where the word first appears.

Pronunciation Key

a	at	ē	me	ô	fork	ü	rule	th	thin
ā	ape	i	in	oi	oil	ů	pull	th	this
ä	far	ī	ice	ou	out	ûr	turn	zh	measure
âr	care	o	hot	u	up	hw	white	ə	about, taken, pencil, lemon, circus
e	end	ō	old	ū	use	ng	song		

A

adobe (ə dō′bē) A brick made of clay that is sometimes mixed with straw and then dried in the sun. (p. 247)

agribusiness (ag′ri biz nis) A large farm owned by a company. (p. 210)

agriculture (ag′ri kul chər) The science and business of growing crops and raising animals. (p. 82)

Allies (al′īz) The countries that fought against the Axis Powers in World War II —Great Britain, France, United States, and the Soviet Union among many others. (p. 55)

aquifer (ak′wə fər) A layer of rock or gravel that traps water underground and supplies wells and springs. (p. 237)

article (är′ti kəl) A story in a newspaper describing an important event that has taken place recently.

artifact (är′tə fakt) An object such as a tool or weapon made by people in the past. (p. 9)

assembly line (ə sem′blē līn) A line of workers and machines used for putting together a product step by step in a factory. (p. 212)

Axis (ak səs) The countries that fought against the Allied Powers in World War II —Germany, Italy, and Japan among many others. (p. 55)

B

bar graph (bär graf) A graph that can be used to show changes over time or changes among different types of information. (p. 205)

basin (bā′sin) A low landform, shaped like a bowl and surrounded by higher land. (p. 74)

bay (bā) A body of water surrounded by land on three sides. (p. 136)

bison (bis ən) A large, shaggy animal with short horns and a hump on its back. (p. 281)

blizzard (bliz′ərd) A heavy snowstorm with very strong winds.

bluegrass (blü'gras) A kind of folk music played on fiddles, banjos, and guitars popular in the Appalachian Mountains. (p. 188)

butte (būt) A flat-topped mountain or hill that stands alone in an area of flat land. (p. 233)

byline (bī'līn) The part of a newspaper article that tells the reader who wrote the story.

C

canal (kə nal') A human-made waterway built for boats and ships to travel through, and for carrying water to places that need it. (p. 36)

canyon (kan'yən) A deep valley with very high, steep sides. (p. 234)

capital resources (kap'i təl rē'sôr sez) The tools, machines, and factories businesses use to produce goods. (p. 101)

checks and balances (cheks and bal'an səz) A system in which the power of each branch of government is balanced by the powers of the other branches. (p. 108)

circle graph (sûr'kəl graf) A graph in the shape of a circle that shows how the different parts of something fit into a whole; also called a pie graph. (p. 173)

citizen (sit'ə zən) A person who was born in a country or who has earned the right to become a member of a country by law. (p. 115)

civil rights (siv'əl rīts) The rights of every citizen to be treated equally under the law. (p. 58)

Civil War (siv'əl wôr) The war between the Union states of the North and the Confederate states of the South, 1861–1865. (p. 41)

climate (klī'mət) The pattern of weather of a certain place over many years. (p. 85)

colony (kol'ə nē) A place that is ruled by another country. (p. 19)

communism (kom'yə niz əm) A system in which business, property, and goods are owned by the government. (p. 57)

conservationist (kon sər vā'shə nist) A person who supports the wise use and protection of natural resources. (p. 279)

constitution (kon sti tu'shən) A plan of government. (p. 108)

consumer (kən sü'mər) A person who buys goods and uses services. (p. 96)

county (koun'tē) One of the sections into which a state or country is divided. (p. 110)

credit (kred'it) A way to purchase something, in which a person borrows money that must be repaid, usually with interest. (p. 102)

culture (kul'chər) The arts, beliefs, and customs that make up a way of life for a group of people. (p. 151)

D

Declaration of Independence (dek lə rā'shən uv in də pen'dəns) A document written in 1776 by colonists telling the world why the colonies wanted independence. (p. 27)

degree (di grē') A unit for measuring distance on Earth's surface. (p. 112)

demand (di mand') The amount of goods and services that consumers are willing and able to buy at certain prices during a given time. (p. 95)

democracy (di mok'rə sē) A system of government in which people elect their leaders. (p. 115)

descendant (di send'ənt) A person who is related to a particular person or group of people who lived long ago. (p. 215)

dialect (dī'ə lekt) A form of a language spoken in a certain place by a certain group of people. (p. 185)

dictator (dik tā'tər) A person who rules a country without sharing power or consulting anyone else. (p. 55)

discrimination (di skrim' ə nā shən) An unfair difference in the way people are treated. (p. 58)

diverse (dī vûrs') Great difference; variety. (p. 153)

drought (drout) A long period of time when there is very little rain or no rain at all. (p. 236)

earthquake (ûrth'kwāk) A shaking of the earth. (p. 266)

economy (i kon'ə mē) The way a country or other place uses or produces natural resources, goods, and services. (p. 82)

editorial (ed' i tôr'ē əl) A newspaper article that offers a personal opinion about a topic.

elevation (el ə vā'shən) The height of land above sea level. (p. 77)

Emancipation Proclamation (i man sə pā'shən prok lə mā'shən) An announcement by President Lincoln in 1863 that all enslaved people living in Confederate states were free. (p. 43)

erosion (i rō'zhən) A wearing away of Earth's surface. (p. 72)

executive branch (eg zek'yə tiv branch) The branch of government that signs bills into laws. (p. 108)

expedition (ek spi dish'ən) A journey of exploration. (p. 34)

fall line (fôl līn) A line joining the waterfalls on numerous rivers where an upland meets a lowland. (p. 138)

federal (fed'ər əl) A system of government that shares power between state, local, and national governments. (p. 115)

fertile (fûr'təl) Land that is able to produce crops and plants easily and plentifully. (p. 200)

frontier (frun tîr') The far edge of a settled area. (p. 38)

fuel (fū'əl) Something used to produce energy. (p. 136)

geyser (gī'zər) A hot, underground spring from which steam and hot water shoot into the air. (p. 267)

glacier (glā'shər) A large mass of ice that moves slowly. (p. 135)

graph (graf) A diagram that represents information. (pp. 105, 173)

grid (grid) A set of squares formed by crisscrossing lines that can help you determine locations, such as on a map or globe. (p. 112)

H

headline (hed'līn) Words printed at the top of an article or story which tell the reader what the story is about.

historian (his tôr'ē ən) A person who studies the past.

human resources (hyü mən rē'sôr sez) All the people employed at a business or organization. (p. 101)

hunter-gatherer (hun'tər gath'ər ər) A person who found food by both hunting animals and gathering plants, fruit, and nuts. (p. 11)

hurricane (hûr'i kān) A storm with very strong winds and heavy rain. (p. 90)

I

immigrant (im'i grənt) A person who comes to a new country to live. (p. 46)

independent (in di pen'dənt) Free from the control of others. (p. 30)

industry (in'də strē) All the businesses that make one kind of product or provide one kind of service. (p. 145)

interdependent (in'tər di pen'dənt) Relying on one another to meet needs and wants. (p. 82)

interest (in'tər ist) Money that is paid for the use of borrowed or deposited money. (p. 102)

interstate highway (in'tər stāt hī'wā) A road with at least two lanes of traffic in each direction that connects two or more states. (p. 270)

invention (in ven'shən) A product that is made for the first time. (p. 47)

investor (in vest'ər) A person or company that uses money to buy something that will make more money. (p. 95)

iron (ī'ərn) A hard metal mainly used to make steel. (p. 208)

irrigation (ir i gā'shən) The use of ditches or pipes to bring water to dry land. (p. 242)

J

jazz (jaz) The form of popular music that grew out of African American culture in the 1920s. (p. 188)

judicial branch (jü dish'əl branch) The branch of government that interprets the laws. (p. 108)

jury (jür'ē) A group of citizens in a court of law who decide if someone accused of a crime is innocent or guilty. (p. 121)

justice (ju'stis) Fair treatment. (p. 124)

kerosene (kar'ə sēn) A fuel made from petroleum. (p. 241)

L

lake effect (lāk i fekt') The effect water has in changing the weather nearby. (p. 88)

large-scale map (lärj skāl map) A map that shows many details in a small area. (p. 141)

latitude (lat'i tüd) A measure of the distance north or south of the equator on Earth. (p. 112)

legislative branch (lej'is lā tiv branch) The branch of government that makes laws. (p. 108)

levee (le'vē) A wall of earth built along a river to keep the river from overflowing onto land. (p. 172)

line graph (līn graf) A graph that shows patterns and amounts of change over time. (pp. 105, 205)

longitude (lon'ji tüd) A measure of distance east or west of the prime meridian on Earth. (p. 112)

Louisiana Purchase (lü ē zē an'ə pûr'chəs) The territory purchased by the United States from France in 1803. (p. 34)

M

magma (mag'ə) Melted rock. (p. 266)

map scale (map scāl) The measurement a map uses to represent real distance on Earth. (p. 141)

mass production (mas prə duk'shən) The process of making large numbers of one product quickly. (p. 212)

megalopolis (meg ə lop'ə lis) A large urban area formed by several cities. (p. 149)

meridian (mə rid'ē ən) A line of longitude; see longitude. (p. 112)

mesa (mā'sə) A hill or mountain with a flat top and steep sides; a high plateau (p. 233)

migration (mī grā'shən) A large movement of people or animals from one place to another (p. 217)

mineral (min'ər əl) A nonrenewable resource found in nature that is not an animal or plant. (p. 71)

mission (mish'ən) A Spanish settlement in the Americas where priests talked about the Christian religion. (p. 18)

mouth (mouth') The place where a river empties into a larger body of water. (p. 167)

municipal (mū nis'ə pəl) Having to do with local or city government. (p. 110)

N

Natural resources (nach'ər əl rē'sôr sez) Materials found in nature that people use. (p. 101)

newspaper (nüz'pā pər) A paper that is usually printed daily or weekly and contains news, opinions, and advertising.

nonrenewable resource (non ri nü'ə bəl rē'sôrs) A thing found in nature that cannot be replaced such as coal. (p. 177)

Northwest Passage (nôrth' west' pas'ij) A water route from Europe to Asia through North America. (p. 19)

O

official document (ə fish'əl dok'yə mənt) A document that contains information that has been agreed upon by one or more people or institutions.

open-pit mining (ō'pən pit mī'ning) A method of removing ore deposits close to the surface of the ground using power shovels. (p. 208)

opportunity cost (opər tū'ni tē kôst) The alternatives that are given up because a particular choice was made. (p. 97)

ore (ôr) A mineral or rock that is mined for the metal or other substance it contains. (p. 208)

P

parallel (par'ə lel) A line of latitude. (p. 112)

patriotism (pā'trē ə tiz'əm) A love for and loyal support of one's country. (p. 123)

peninsula (pə nin'sə lə) Land that has water on three sides. (p. 168)

petroleum (pə trō'lē əm) A fuel, commonly called oil, that forms underground from dead plants. (p. 176)

pioneer (pī ə nîr') A person who leads the way or one who settles a new part of the country. (p. 217)

plateau (pla tō') An area of flat land, higher than the surrounding country. (p. 74)

population density (pop ū lā'shən den'sə tē) A measurement of how many people live in a particular area; a type of map that shows the same. (p. 238)

population distribution (pop ū lā'shən dis trə bū'shən) A measurement of where in an area people live; a type of map that shows the same. (p. 238)

powwow (pou'wou) A Native American festival. (p. 252)

prairie (prâr'ē) Flat or rolling land covered with grass. (p. 202)

precipitation (pri sip i tā'shən) The moisture that falls to the ground in the form of rain, sleet, hail, or snow. (p. 86)

prehistory (prē his'tōr ē) The time before written records. (p. 9)

primary source (prī'mer ē sôrs) An artifact, photograph, or eyewitness account of an event in the past.

prime meridian (prīm mə rid'ē ən) The line of longitude, marked 0°, from which other meridians are numbered. (p. 112)

producer (prə dū'sər) A person or company that makes or creates something. (p. 100)

profit (prof'it) The money a business earns after it pays for tools, salaries, and other costs. (p. 94)

pueblo (pweb' lō) Native American town or village with adobe and stone houses; any Native American group or people who live or whose ancestors lived in adobe or stone houses usually in the Southwest United States. (p. 247)

R

rain shadow (rān shad'ō) The side of the mountain that is usually dry because precipitation falls on the other side. (p. 87)

Reconstruction (rē kən struk'shən) The period after the Civil War in which Congress passed laws designed to rebuild the country and bring the Southern states back into the Union. (p. 44)

refinery (ri fī'nə rē) A factory which turns crude oil into useful products such as heating oil, gasoline, plastics, and paint. (p. 176)

region (rē'jen) An area, or group of states, with common features that set it apart from other areas. (p. 79)

renewable resource (ri nü' ə bəl rē'sôrs) A natural resource that can be replaced, such as trees or water. (p. 176)

reservation (rez ûr vā'shən) Land set aside by the government as settlements for Native Americans. (p. 119)

resource (rē' sôrs') A person, thing, or material that can be used for help or support. (p. 10)

revolution (rev ə lü'shən) The overthrow of a government. (p. 25)

road map (rōd map) A map that shows roads. (p. 270)

rodeo (rōd ē ō) A rodeo is a show that has contests in horseback riding, roping, and other similar skills. (p. 285)

rule of law (rool əv lô) The belief that a country's laws apply to all of its people equally. (p. 124)

S

sea level (sē lev'əl) The level of the surface of the sea. (p. 77)

secondary source (sek'ən der e sôrs) An account of an event from a person who did not see or experience it.

segregation (seg ri gā'shən) The practice of keeping racial groups separate. (p. 186)

service (sûr'vis) Something that is done to help another person. (p. 146)

silicon (sil i kän) A material used in the manufacture of computer chips. (p. 244)

small-scale map (smôl skāl map) A map that shows few details of a large area. (p. 141)

solar energy (sō'lər en'ər jē) Energy that comes from the sun. (p. 244)

source (sôrs) The starting point of a river. (p. 167)

sovereign (sov'ər in) A nation or group of people not controlled by others; independent. (p. 119)

suburban (sə bûr'bən) Describes a community near a city. (p. 149)

suffrage (suf'rij) The right to vote. (p. 51)

supply (sə plī) The amount of an item available at certain prices during a given time. (p. 95)

T

tax (taks) Money people and businesses must pay to the government so that it can provide public services. (p. 25)

technology (tek nol'ə jē) The use of skills, tools, and machines to meet people's needs; new method of doing something. (p. 13)

telecommunications (tel'i kə mū ni kā' shənz) The technology that allows people to send messages and images long distances quickly. (p. 276)

territory (ter'i tôr'ē) Land owned by a country either within or outside the country's borders. (p. 33)

terrorism (ter'ə riz əm) The use of violence and threats to acheive a political goal. (p. 60)

timberline (tim'bər līn) A tree line. (p. 268)

tornado (tôr nā'dō) A powerful wind storm with a funnel-shaped cloud that moves quickly over land. (p. 90)

tourist (tur'ist) A person who is traveling for pleasure. (p. 140)

tradition (trə dish'ən) A custom that is passed down from parents to their children. This includes festivals, songs, and dances. (p. 219)

tributary (trib'yə ter ē) A river or stream that flows into a larger river. (p. 73)

U

urban (ûr'bən) A city and its surrounding areas. (p. 148)

V

veto (vē'tō) The power of the executive branch to reject a bill passed by the legislature. (p. 109)

W

wetland (wet'land) A low flat area covered with water. (p. 167)

Index

This index lists many topics that appear in the book, along with the pages on which they are found. Page numbers after a *c* refer you to a chart or diagram, after a *g*, to a graph, after an *m*, to a map, after a *p*, to a photograph or picture, and after a *q*, to a quotation.

E

Credits

Illustration Credits :10: (tl) Steve Chorney, 14-15: Christian Hook. 17: Yuen Lee. 70-71: Gary Overacre.71: (b) Dan Trush. 86-87: Peter Bull. 88: Peter Bull. 100: Robert Papp. 104: Ken Batelman. 107: Ken Batelman. 108: Ken Batelman.

Photo Credits: All Photographs are by Macmillan/McGraw-Hill (MMH) except as noted below.

Volume 1: iv: (bl) Bill Silliker, Jr./Animals Animals. iv-vi: (bkgd) Bob Pool/Getty Images. Vii: (c) Owaki - Kulla/Corbis. Vi-vii: (bkgd) Macduff Everton/Corbis.

COV (bl)Bettmann/ CORBIS, (br)SW Productions/Brand X/ CORBIS, (t)Maria Ferrari/SuperStock; TTLPG SW Productions/Brand X/ CORBIS; GH-GH1 Joseph Sohm/Visions of America/ CORBIS; GH2 (t)Charles Smith/ CORBIS, (b)Ken Straiton/ CORBIS; GH3 (t)Iconotec/Alamy Images, (c)Mark Richards/PhotoEdit, (b)Gibson Stock Photography; R2-R3 MMH; R5 E.R. Degginger/Dembinsky Photo Associates; RF (t)CORBIS, (c)The Granger Collection, New York, (b)Stockdisc/ Getty Images; iv Bill Silliker, Jr./Animals Animals; iv-v (bkgd)Bob Pool/Getty Images; vi Owaki - Kulla/ CORBIS; viii (bg)Joe Sohm/The Image Works, Inc., (inset)Map Resources; vi-vii Macduff Everton/ CORBIS; 1 Cade Martin/age footstock; 2 (tl)Art Resource, Inc, (tr)Dennis Degnan/ CORBIS, (bl)Flip Schulke/ CORBIS, (br)AP Images; 3 (tr)National Geographic Image Collection, (tl)Carolyn Kaster/AP Images, (bl)Richard T. Nowitz/ CORBIS, (br)AP Images; 4-5 (bg)Erin Patrice O'Brien/Getty Images; 5 (cr)purestock/PunchStock, (tr)[Detail] Photo by Henry Clay Anderson © NMAAHC/Smithsonian Institution, (bl)R.Nowitz/Photri-Microstock; 6 (cl)MMH, (cr)"Coronado's Expedition", Courtesy of Abell-Hanger Foundation and of the Permian Basin Petroleum Museum, Library and Hall of Fame of Midland, Texas where this painting is on permanent display.; 8 (bcr)The Granger Collection, New York; 8-9 (LesOp)MMH; 9 Werner Forman/Art Resource, Inc.; 10 (tr)MMH; 10-11 (bkgd)MMH; 12 (cl)Marilyn Angel Wynn/Nativestock Pictures; 12-13 (bg)George H. H. Huey Photography; 13 (c)The Granger Collection, New York; 14 (cl)Richard A. Cooke/ CORBIS; 14-15 (bkgd)MMH; 15 (tr)Steve Kaufman/Peter Arnold, Inc.; 16 (bl)Image courtesy of NASA/Kennedy Space Center, (bcl)"Coronado's Expedition", Courtesy of Abell-Hanger Foundation and of the Permian Basin Petroleum Museum, Library and Hall of Fame of Midland, Texas where this painting is on permanent display., (bcr)Collection of the New-York Historical Society, USA/Bridgeman Art Library, (br)Artist Robert Griffing and his publisher Paramount Press Inc.; 16-17 (LesOp)Image courtesy of NASA/Kennedy Space Center; 17 (br)MMH, (t)FoodCollection/Index Stock Imagery; 18 (tl)R. Krubner/Robertstock.com; 18-19 (bg)"Coronado's Expedition", Courtesy of Abell-Hanger Foundation and of the Permian Basin Petroleum Museum, Library and Hall of Fame of Midland, Texas where this painting is on permanent display.; 19 (tr)The Granger Collection, New York; 20 (cl)AP Images; 20-21 (bg)Collection of the New-York Historical Society, USA/Bridgeman Art Library; 21 (tr)The Granger Collection, New York; 22-23 (bg)Artist Robert Griffing and his publisher Paramount Press Inc.; 23 (tr)Bettmann/ CORBIS, (c)Image courtesy of NASA/Kennedy Space Center; 24 (bl)Culver Pictures/The Art Archive, (bcl)The Granger Collection, New York, (bcr)SuperStock, (br)The Granger Collection, New York; 24-25 (LesOp)Culver Pictures/The Art Archive; 25 The Colonial Williamsburg Foundation; 26 (t)Dennis Degnan/ CORBIS; 26-27 (bg)The Granger Collection, New York; 27 (t)Library of Congress; 28 (t)North Wind Picture Archives, (bl)Joe Raedle/Getty Images; 28-29 (bg)Lee Foster/Alamy Images; 29 (br)James Lemass/Index Stock Imagery, (t)SuperStock; 30 (t)Bettmann/ CORBIS; 30-31 (bg)The Granger Collection, New York; 31 (c)James Lemass/Index Stock Imagery; 32 (bl)The Granger Collection, New York, (bcl)Painting: "Lewis and Clark: The Departure from the Wood River Encampment, May 14, 1804" by Gary R. Lucy. Courtesy of the Gary R. Lucy Gallery, Inc., Washington, MO, (bcr)The Granger Collection, New York, (br)MPI/Hulton Archive/Getty Images; 32-33 (LesOp)The Granger Collection, New York; 33 Artist Robert Griffing and his publisher Paramount Press Inc.; 34 (cl)MMH; 34-35 (bg)Macduff Everton/Iconica/Getty Images; 35 (c)Painting: "Lewis and Clark: The Departure from the Wood River Encampment, May 14, 1804" by Gary R. Lucy. Courtesy of the Gary R. Lucy Gallery, Inc., Washington, MO; 36 (tl)The Granger Collection, New York; 36-37 (bg)Bettmann/ CORBIS; 37 (t)The Granger Collection, New York; 38 (t)D. Boone/ CORBIS; 38-39 (bg)MPI/Hulton Archive/Getty Images; 39 (t)Bettmann/ CORBIS, (c)MPI/Hulton Archive/Getty Images; 40 (bl) CORBIS, (bcl)From the original painting by Mort Künstler,The Angle © 1988 Mort Künstler, Inc. www.mkunstler.com/Künstler Enterprises, (bcr)The Granger Collection, New York, (br)Scala/Art Resource, Inc.; 40-41 (LesOp)The Granger Collection, New York; 41 (b) CORBIS, (t)The Granger Collection, New York; 42 (t)The Granger Collection, New York; 42-43 (bg)From the original painting by Mort Künstler,The Angle © 1988 Mort Künstler, Inc. www.mkunstler.com/Künstler Enterprises; 43 (t)Private Collection/Bridgeman Art Library; 44-45 The Granger Collection, New York; 46 (t)Michael Freeman/IPNstock; 46-47 (bg)Scala/Art Resource, Inc.; 47 (t)From the original painting by Mort Künstler,The Angle © 1988 Mort Künstler, Inc. www.mkunstler.com/Künstler Enterprises; 48 (bl)The Granger Collection, New York, (bcl)The Granger Collection, New York, (bcr)Bettmann/ CORBIS, (br)The Granger Collection, New York; 48-49 (LesOp)AP Images; 49 (br)The Granger Collection, New York, (tr)Visions of America, LLC/ Alamy Images; 50 Swim Ink 2, LLC/ CORBIS; 50-51 (c)The Granger Collection, New York; 51 (t)Bettmann/ CORBIS; 52 (t)Bettmann/ CORBIS; 52-53 (bg) CORBIS; 53 (t)The Granger Collection, New York; 54 (inset)David J. & Janice L. Frent Collection/ CORBIS; 54-55 (bg)The Granger Collection, New York; 55 (t)AP Images, (c)The Granger Collection, New York; 56 (c)Car Culture/Getty Images, (bl)Neil Armstrong, NASA/AP Images, (bc)Francis Miller/Time Life Pictures/Getty Images, (br)Terry W. Eggers/ CORBIS; 56-57 (LesOp)Hulton Archive/Getty Images; 57 Historicus, Inc; 58-59 (bg)Francis Miller/Time Life Pictures/Getty Images; 59 (t)Neil Armstrong, NASA/AP Images; 60 (t)David Parker/Photo Researchers, Inc., (b) Matthew McDermott/CORBIS; 60-61 (bg)Terry W. Eggers/ CORBIS; 61 (c)Jim West/The Image Works, Inc., (bl)Francis Miller/Time Life Pictures/Getty Images; 62 (c)Werner Forman/Art Resource, Inc.; 64 (t)David Roth/Riser/Getty Images; 65 (UnitOp)Joseph Sohm; Visions of America/ CORBIS; 66 (t)The Granger Collection, New York, (tr)Bass Photo Co. Collection/Indiana Historical Society, (bl)The Albuquerque Journal/Jeff Geissler, (br)Alex Wong/ Getty Images; 67 (tl)Bruce Ackerman/Star-Banner/Silver Image Photo Agency, (tr)Hamad I Mohammed/Reuters/ CORBIS,(br)Charles O'Rear/ CORBIS, (bl)Andre Jenny/Alamy Images; 68 (tr)Wallace Garrison/Index Stock Imagery/ Jupiterimages, (br)Amanda Clement/Photodisc/PunchStock, (cl)Tony Souter/ Dorling Kindersley Ltd. Picture Library; 69 (br)Jerry Young/Dorling Kindersley Ltd. Picture Library, (tr)Roy Ooms/Masterfile, (tc)Charles Pefley/Mira.com; 70 (bl)MMH, (bcl)Jerry and Marcy Monkman/Danita Delimont Stock Photography, (bcr)Craig Tuttle/ CORBIS, (br)Bill Silliker, Jr./Animals Animals; 70-71 (LesOp)MMH; 71 (b)MMH; 72-73 (bg)Jerry and Marcy Monkman/Danita Delimont Stock Photography; 74 (cr)Craig Tuttle/ CORBIS, (bl)Harvey Lloyd/Getty Images; 74-75 (bg)Macduff Everton/ CORBIS; 75 (cl)Sime s.a.s./eStock Photo/eStock Photo, (bl)Douglas Peebles/ CORBIS, (br)Mary Van de Ven/Pacific Stock; 76 (b)Bill Silliker, Jr./Animals Animals, (c)Craig Tuttle/ CORBIS; 78 (bl)David Bacon/ The Image Works, Inc., (bc)Theo Allofs/Visuals Unlimited, (br)Matt Meadows/ Peter Arnold, Inc.; 78-79 (LesOp)Robert Frerck/Getty Images; 79 David Bacon/ The Image Works, Inc.; 80 (c)Theo Allofs/Visuals Unlimited; 80-81 (bg)Robert J. Hurt Landscape Photography; 82 (inset)Matt Meadows/Peter Arnold, Inc.; 82-83 (bg)Adam Jones/Visuals Unlimited; 83 (c)Robert Frerck/Getty Images; 84 (bcr)MMH, (bl)Bob Pool/Getty Images, (bcl)David Young-Wolff/PhotoEdit, (br)Stocktrek Images/Alamy Images; 84-85 (LesOp)Bob Pool/Getty Images; 86 (bl)David Young-Wolff/PhotoEdit; 86-87 (bkgd)MMH; 88 (c)MMH; 90 (c)Jim West/ Alamy; 90-91 (bg)Carsten Peter/National Geographic/Getty Images; 91 (c)David Young-Wolff/PhotoEdit; 92 (bl)Scott Indermaur for MMH, (bc)Scott Indermaur for MMH, (br)Richard Hutchings/Digital Light Source; 92-93 (LesOp)Scott Indermaur for MMH; 93 (bkgd)Scott Indermaur for MMH, (c)Scott Indermaur for MMH, (bkgd)Scott Indermaur for MMH; 94 (b)Scott Indermaur for MMH; 95 (t)Scott Indermaur for MMH, (c)Scott Indermaur for MMH; 96 (cr)Richard Hutchings/ Digital Light Source, (bkgd)Scott Indermaur for MMH; 97 (tl)Scott Indermaur for MMH, (bg)Guy Grenier/Masterfile, (cr)Scott Indermaur for MMH; 98 (br)MMH, (bl)AP Images, (bcl)Richard Hamilton Smith/ CORBIS, (bcr)Bill Aron/PhotoEdit; 98-99 (LesOp)Andreas Pollok/Getty Images; 99 AP Images; 100 (t)MMH; 100 (b)Michael Newman/PhotoEdit, (t)Richard Hamilton Smith/ CORBIS, (c)Paul Thompson/Danita Delimont Stock Photography; 102 (c)Bill Aron/PhotoEdit, (bg)Tetra Images/PunchStock; 102-103 (bg)Tetra Images/PunchStock; 103 (c)Michael Newman/PhotoEdit, (bg)Tetra Images/PunchStock; 104 (tl)MMH, (c)Bill Aron/PhotoEdit; 106 (bl)Blue Shadows/Alamy Images, (br)Dennis MacDonald/PhotoEdit, (bc)John Elk III/Bruce Coleman Inc.; 106-107 (LesOp)Blue Shadows/Alamy Images; 107 (r)MMH; 108 (l)John Elk III/Bruce Coleman Inc., (c)Bizuayehu Tesfaye/AP Images, (r)John RunningSABA/Social Security Shoot/ John Running Photographs; 109 (c)MMH; 110 (b)Dennis MacDonald/PhotoEdit, (t)Mike Segar/Reuters/ CORBIS; 110-111 (bg)Gibson Stock Photography; 111 (tr)Katy Lloyd/King William County, (cr)Blue Shadows/Alamy Images; 114 (bl)Anne Cusack/Pool/Reuters/ CORBIS, (bc)Mark Reinstein/The Image Works, Inc., (br)Dan Budnik/Woodfin Camp & Associates; 114-115 (LesOp)Joe Sohm/The Image Works, Inc.; 115 Anne Cusack/Pool/Reuters/ CORBIS, (inset)PunchStock; 116 (c)Mark Reinstein/The Image Works, Inc.; 116-117 (bg)Map Resources; 117 (t)Larry Downing/Reuters/Landov, (b)Mark Wilson/Getty Images; 118 (t)Henry k Kaiser/eStock Photo, (b)Shehzad Noorani - Woodfin Camp/IPNstock; 119 (t)Dan Budnik/Woodfin Camp & Associates, (c)Mark Reinstein/The Image Works, Inc.; 120 (bl)BL Images Ltd/Alamy Images, (bc)LWA-Dann Tardif/ CORBIS, (br)Flip Schulke/ CORBIS; 120-121 (LesOp)BL Images Ltd/Alamy Images; 121 Bettmann/ CORBIS; 122 AP Images; 123 (tl)LWA-Dann Tardif/ CORBIS, (br)Jeff Greenberg/ PhotoEdit; 124 Stock Connection Blue/Alamy Images; 125 (t)Flip Schulke/ CORBIS, (b)BL Images Ltd/Alamy Images; 126 (tr)The McGraw-Hill Companies, Inc./Emily and David Tietz, photographers, (c)Tetra Images/PunchStock; BKCOV Maria Ferrari/SuperStock.

ACKNOWLEDGMENTS

Grateful acknowledgment is given to the following authors and publishers. Every effort has been made to trace the ownership of all copyrighted material and to secure the necessary permissions to reprint these selections. In the case of some selections for which acknowledgment is not given, extensive research has failed to locate the copyright holders.